The
WORST-CASE SCENARIO
Survival Handbook

By Joshua Piven and David Borgenicht

CHRONICLE BOOKS

SAN FRANCISCO

The authors wish to thank all the experts
who contributed to the making of this book,
as well as Jay Schaefer, Laura Lovett, Steve
Mockus, and the entire team at Chronicle Books.

Library of Congress Cataloging-in-Publication Data available.

ISBN 0-8118-2555-8

Printed in the United States of America

Designed by book soup publishing, inc.

Typeset in Adobe Caslon, Bundesbahn Pi, and Zapf Dingbats

Illustrations by Brenda Brown

a book soup publishing book

Distributed in Canada by Raincoast Books
9050 Shaughnessy Street
Vancouver, British Columbia V6P 6E5

20 19 18 17 16 15

Chronicle Books LLC
85 Second Street
San Francisco, California 94105

www.chroniclebooks.com

THE WORST-CASE SCENARIO
Survival Handbook

WARNING

When a life is imperiled or a dire situation is at hand, safe alternatives may not exist. To deal with the worst-case scenarios presented in this book, we highly recommend—insist, actually—that the best course of action is to consult a professionally trained expert. DO NOT ATTEMPT TO UNDERTAKE ANY OF THE ACTIVITIES DESCRIBED IN THIS BOOK YOURSELF. But because highly trained professionals may not always be available when the safety of individuals is at risk, we have asked experts on various subjects to describe the techniques they might employ in those emergency situations. THE PUBLISHER, AUTHORS, AND EXPERTS DISCLAIM ANY LIABILITY from any injury that may result from the use, proper or improper, of the information contained in this book. All the information in this book comes directly from experts in the situation at hand, but we do not guarantee that the information contained herein is complete, safe, or accurate, nor should it be considered a substitute for your good judgment and common sense. And finally, nothing in this book should be construed or interpreted to infringe on the rights of other persons or to violate criminal statutes: we urge you to obey all laws and respect all rights, including property rights, of others.

—The Authors

CONTENTS

FOREWORD

THE RULES OF SURVIVAL
By "Mountain" Mel Deweese

I am a Survival Evasion Resistance Escape Instructor. I have developed, written, attended, and taught courses around the world to more than 100,000 students—civilians, naval aviators, and elite Navy SEAL teams. I have more than 30 years of survival training experience, from the Arctic Circle to the Canadian wilderness, from the jungles of the Philippines to the Australian desert.

Let's just say that I've learned a few things about survival over the years.

Whatever the situation, whether you're out in the mountains, on board a plane, or driving cross-country, to "survive" means "To outlive, to remain alive or in existence; live on. To continue to exist or live after." After all, that's what it's really all about—about continuing to exist, no matter how dire the circumstances.

• You have to be prepared—mentally, physically, and equipment-wise.

I would have to call my training in the

Arctic Circle the ultimate survival adventure. The Arctic is an extremely harsh and unforgiving environment, and yet the Inuit people (Eskimos) not only survive, they live here at the top of the world. Most of the items you need for Arctic survival must come with you when you go— the Arctic offers little for improvisation.

One morning, as we huddled inside our igloo drinking tea to warm up, I noticed that our senior Inuit guide drank several more cups of tea than the rest of us. "He must be thirsty," I thought. We then proceeded outside for our morning trek across the frozen landscape. After we reached our camp, the senior instructor walked over to a small knoll. Our young Inuit guide interpreted his words: "This is where the fox will come to seek a high lookout point. This is a good place to set a trap." The older man then took out his steel trap, set it, laid out the chain, and to my surprise, urinated upon the end of the chain!

The younger instructor explained: "That's why he drank all that tea this morning—to anchor it!" Indeed, the chain had frozen securely to the ground.

The lesson: Resources and improvisation equals survival.

the worst-case scenario survival handbook

• You must not ignore the importance of the mental aspects of survival; in particular, you must stay calm and you must not panic. And remember that willpower is the most crucial survival skill of all—don't catch that terrible disease of "Give-up-itis." All these mental strengths especially come into play when someone makes a mistake—which is inevitable.

One trip into the jungles of the Philippines, our old guide Gunny selected and gathered various plants while we were trekking. Upon arrival at the camp, Gunny skillfully prepared bamboo to use for cooking tubes. To these he added leaves, snails (he claimed only the old men catch snails because they are slow—young men catch fast shrimp), and a few slices of green mango. He also added a few things I could not discern. Topping this off with leaves from the taro plant, he added water and placed the bamboo cooking tube on the fire.

After the jungle feast, we settled into the darkness for sleep. During the night, I experienced pain, contraction, and itching in my throat. We were in pitch darkness, far from civilization, and my airways were progressively closing. The following morning, the condition worsened and my breathing was becoming restricted. I questioned the instructor, and he agreed he had the same problem. That we shared our distress was reassuring and it led to our determining the source of the problem. It turned out we had not boiled the taro leaves long enough. Recovering hours later, I mentally logged this as a lesson learned the hard way: Even the old man of the jungle can make mistakes.

We all make mistakes. Overcoming them is survival as well.

• You must have a survival plan. And your plan should consider the following essential elements: food, fire, water, and shelter, as well as signals and first aid.

I remember a military survival training course I took in another jungle. A tropical environment is one of the easiest to survive, if you know where to look. It offers all of the needs for survival— food, fire, water, shelter. We needed water badly but could not head for the major streams, rivers, or bodies of water to quench our thirst, as the "enemy" was tracking us. The enemy knew our dire need for water, and he would be watching those areas. Looking into the jungle foliage, our guide Pepe pulled his jungle bolo (a large knife) from its wooden case and pointed to a thick, grapelike vine, 3-4 inches in diameter. He cut the vine at the top, then sliced off a 2-3 foot section, motioned to me, and held it above my parched lips. Excellent! In total, it produced almost a large glass of water. Then he cut into a rattan vine that provided nearly the same amount.

That evening we tapped into the trunk of a *taboy* tree, placed bamboo tube reservoirs we had constructed beneath the tap, and left them overnight. Early the next morning, I was surprised to find 6-8 quarts of water in our reservoirs.

The next morning in the rain, Pepe stopped to cut a tall bundle of grass. He selected a smooth-barked tree and wrapped the grass around the tree to form a spigot. He then placed his bamboo drinking cup under the grass spigot. I was not convinced about the quality of his filter, but it was a good way for us to gather rainwater. That night, after we had reached the safe area, the jungle darkness fell upon us and we sat in the flicker of the bamboo fire. Pepe smiled at me and said, "Once again we've evaded the enemy and learned to return."

That simple phrase became our motto—and in fact, is the motto of every survival trainer, whether or not they know it. "Learn to return."

This guide might help you do just that.

PREFACE

Anything that can go wrong will.
—Murphy's Law

Be prepared.
—Boy Scout motto

The principle behind this book is a simple one: You just never know.

You never really know what curves life will throw at you, what is lurking around the corner, what is hovering above, what is swimming beneath the surface. You never know when you might to be called upon to perform an act of extreme bravery and to choose life or death with your own actions.

But when you are called, we want to be sure that you know what to do. And that is why we wrote this book. We want you to know what to do when the pilots pass out and you have to land the plane. We want you to know what to do when you see that shark fin heading toward you. We want you to know how to make fire in the wilderness without any matches. We want you to know what to do in these and in dozens of other life-threatening situations, from being forced to jump from a bridge to being forced to jump from a car, from taking a punch correctly to outsmarting a charging bull, and from escaping a sniper to treating a bullet wound.

We were not survival experts ourselves when we undertook this project—just regular, everyday folk like you. Joshua grew up in the East—a street-smart city boy. David grew up in the West and spent his youth hiking and camping and fishing (even though his family used a Volkswagen van most of the time). We were just a couple of inquisitive journalists from different backgrounds who worried a lot and were interested in knowing how to survive a variety of crisis situations, likely or unlikely (mostly the latter). Together, we consulted experts in a variety of fields to compile the handbook you have before you. The information in this book comes directly from dozens of expert sources—stuntmen, physicians, EMT instructors, bomb squad officers, bullfighters, survival experts, scuba instructors, demolition derby drivers, locksmiths, sky divers, alligator farmers, marine biologists, and avalanche rescue patrol members, to name a few.

Within this book, you will find simple, step-by-step instructions for dealing with 40 life- and limb-threatening situations, with instructive illustrations throughout. We've also provided other essential tips and information—marked with red bullets—that you must know. Any and each of them could save your life. Ever wonder how you would deal with the kinds of situations that usually only come up when you are a movie action hero? Now you can find out. And then, like the Boy Scouts, you too will be prepared.

So keep this book on hand at all times. It is informative and entertaining, but useful, too. Get a copy and keep it in your glove compartment. Take it with you when you travel. Give a copy to your friends and loved ones. Because the Boy Scouts know what they're talking about.

And you just never know.

—Joshua Piven and David Borgenicht

CHAPTER I

GREAT ESCAPES
AND ENTRANCES

HOW TO ESCAPE FROM QUICKSAND

1 When walking in quicksand country, carry a stout pole—it will help you get out should you need to.

2 As soon as you start to sink, lay the pole on the surface of the quicksand.

3 Flop onto your back on top of the pole. After a minute or two, equilibrium in the quicksand will be achieved, and you will no longer sink.

4 Work the pole to a new position: under your hips and at right angles to your spine. The pole will keep your hips from sinking, as you (slowly) pull out first one leg and then the other.

5 Take the shortest route to firmer ground, moving slowly.

How to Avoid Sinking

Quicksand is just ordinary sand mixed with upwelling water, which makes it behave like a liquid. However, quicksand—unlike water—does not easily let go. If you try to pull a limb out of quicksand, you have to work against the vacuum left behind. Here are a few tips:

- The viscosity of quicksand increases with shearing—move slowly so the viscosity is as low as possible.
- Floating on quicksand is relatively easy and is the best way to avoid its clutches. You are more buoyant in quicksand than you are in water. Humans are less dense than freshwater, and saltwater is slightly more dense. Floating is easier in saltwater than freshwater and much easier in quicksand. Spread your arms and legs far apart and try to float on your back.

When in an area with quicksand, bring a stout pole and use it to put your back into a floating position.

Place the pole at a right angle from your spine to keep your hips afloat.

HOW TO BREAK DOWN A DOOR

INTERIOR DOORS

1 Give the door a well-placed kick or two to the lock area to break it down.

Running at the door and slamming against it with your shoulder or body is not usually as effective as kicking with your foot. Your foot exerts more force than your shoulder, and you will be able to direct this force toward the area of the locking mechanism more succinctly with your foot.

**Alternate Method
(if you have a screwdriver)**

Look on the front of the doorknob for a small hole or keyhole.

Most interior doors have what are called privacy sets. These locks are usually installed on bedrooms and bathrooms and can be locked from the inside when the door is shut, but have an emergency access hole in the center of the door handle which allows entry to the locking mechanism inside. Insert the screwdriver or probe into the handle and push the locking mechanism, or turn the mechanism to open the lock.

EXTERIOR DOORS

If you are trying to break down an exterior door, you will need more force. Exterior doors are of sturdier construction and are designed with security in mind, for obvious reasons. In general, you can expect to see two kinds of latches on outside doors: a passage- or entry-lock set for latching and a dead-bolt lock for security. The passage set is used for keeping the door from swinging open and does not lock. The entry-lock set utilizes a dead latch and can be locked before closing the door.

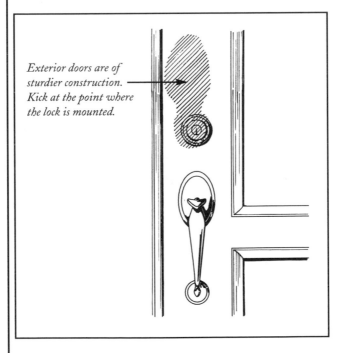

Exterior doors are of sturdier construction. Kick at the point where the lock is mounted.

1 Give the door several well-placed kicks at the point where the lock is mounted.

An exterior door usually takes several tries to break down this way, so keep at it.

Alternate Method
(if you have a sturdy piece of steel)

⭐ Wrench or pry the lock off the door by inserting the tool between the lock and the door and prying back and forth.

Alternate Method
(if you have a screwdriver, hammer, and awl)

⭐ Remove the pins from the hinges (if the door opens toward you) and then force the door open from the hinge side.

Get a screwdriver or an awl and a hammer. Place the awl or screwdriver underneath the hinge, with the pointy end touching the end of the bolt or screw. Using the hammer, strike the other end of the awl or screwdriver until the hinge comes out.

ASSESSING AMOUNT OF FORCE REQUIRED

Interior doors in general are of a lighter construction than exterior doors and usually are thinner—$1^3/_8''$ thick to $1^5/_8''$ thick—than exterior doors, which generally are $1^3/_4''$ thick. In general, older homes will be more likely to have solid wood doors, while newer ones will have the cheaper, hollow core models. Knowing what type of door you are dealing with will help you determine how to break it down. You can usually determine the construction and solidity of a door by tapping on it.

HOLLOW CORE. This type is generally used for interior doors, since it provides no insulation or security, and requires minimal force. These doors can often be opened with a screwdriver.

SOLID WOOD. These are usually oak or some other hardwood, and require an average amount of force and a crowbar or other similar tool.

SOLID CORE. These have a softwood inner frame with a laminate on each side and a chipped or shaved wood core, and require an average amount of force and a screwdriver.

METAL CLAD. These are usually softwood with a thin metal covering, and require average or above average force and a crowbar.

HOLLOW METAL. These doors are of a heavier gauge metal that usually has a reinforcing channel around the edges and the lock mounting area, and are sometimes filled with some type of insulating material. These require maximum force and a crowbar.

HOW TO BREAK INTO A CAR

Most cars that are more than ten years old have vertical, push-button locks. These are locks that come straight out of the top of the car door and have rods that are set vertically inside the door. These locks can be easily opened with a wire hanger or a SlimJim, or picked, as described below. Newer cars have horizontal locks, which emerge from the side of the car door and are attached to horizontal lock rods. These are more difficult to manipulate without a special tool but can also be picked.

HOW TO BREAK INTO A CAR WITH A HANGER

1 Take a wire hanger and bend it into a long J.

2 Square off the bottom of the J so the square is $1\frac{1}{2}$ to 2 inches wide (see illustration).

3 Slide the hanger into the door, between the window and the weather stripping.
Open the door by feel and by trial and error. Feel for the end of the button rod and, when you have it, pull it up to open the lock.

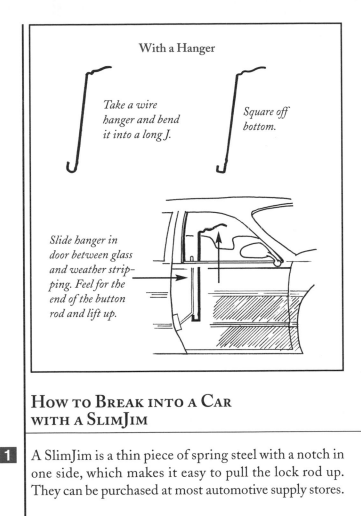

With a Hanger

Take a wire hanger and bend it into a long J.

Square off bottom.

Slide hanger in door between glass and weather stripping. Feel for the end of the button rod and lift up.

How to Break into a Car with a SlimJim

1 A SlimJim is a thin piece of spring steel with a notch in one side, which makes it easy to pull the lock rod up. They can be purchased at most automotive supply stores.

Slide the tool gently between the window and the weather stripping.

Some cars will give you only a quarter of an inch of access to the lock linkage, so go slowly and be patient.

2 Do not jerk the tool trying to find the lock rod. This can break the lock linkage, and on auto-locks it can easily rip the wires in the door.

3 Move the tool back and forth until it grabs the lock rod and then gently move it until the lock flips over.

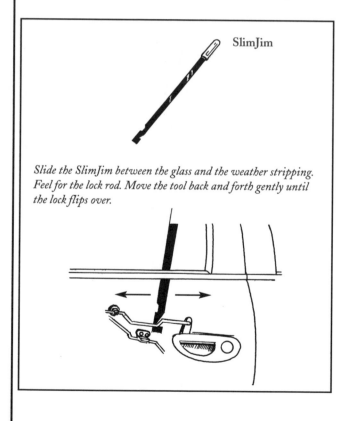

SlimJim

Slide the SlimJim between the glass and the weather stripping. Feel for the lock rod. Move the tool back and forth gently until the lock flips over.

How to Pick a Car Lock

1 You will need two tools—one to manipulate the pins or wafers inside the lock core and one to turn the cylinder.

You can use a small Allen wrench to turn the lock and a long bobby pin to move the pins and wafers. Keep in mind that many car locks are harder to pick than door locks. They often have a small shutter that covers and protects the lock, and this can make the process more difficult.

2 While the bobby pin is in the lock, exert constant and light turning pressure with the wrench.

This is the only way to discern if the pins or wafers—which line up with the notches and grooves in a key—are lined up correctly. Most locks have five pins.

3 Move the bobby pin to manipulate the pins or wafers until you feel the lock turn smoothly.

Alternate Method

Use a key from a different car from the same manufacturer.

There are surprisingly few lock variations, and the alien key may just work.

Be Aware

We of course assume you are seeking to enter your own car.

HOW TO
HOT-WIRE A CAR

Hot-wiring a car without the owner's permission is illegal, except in repossessions. Hot-wiring can be dangerous; there is a risk of electrical shock. Hot-wiring will not work on all cars, particularly cars with security devices. Some "kill switches" can prevent hot-wiring.

1 Open the hood.

2 Locate the coil wire (it is red).
To find it, follow the plug wires, which lead to the coil wire. The plug and coil wires are located at the rear of the engine on most V-8s. On six-cylinder engines, the wires are on the left side near the center of the engine, and on four-cylinder engines, they are located on the right side near the center of the engine.

3 Run a wire from the positive (+) side of the battery to the positive side of the coil, or the red wire that goes to the coil.
This step gives power to the dash, and the car will not run unless it is performed first.

4 Locate the starter solenoid.
On most GM cars, it is on the starter. On Fords, it is located on the left-side (passenger-side) fender well.

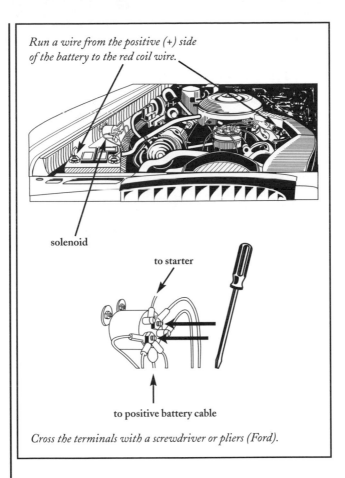

Run a wire from the positive (+) side of the battery to the red coil wire.

solenoid

to starter

to positive battery cable

Cross the terminals with a screwdriver or pliers (Ford).

An easy way to find it is to follow the positive battery cable. You will see a small wire and the positive battery cable. Cross the two with a screwdriver or pliers. This cranks the engine.

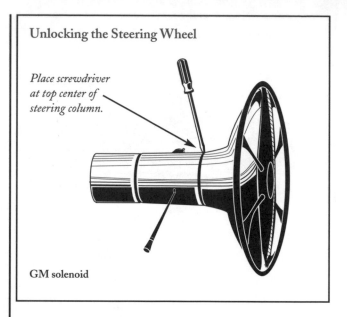

Unlocking the Steering Wheel

Place screwdriver at top center of steering column.

GM solenoid

5 If the car has a standard transmission, make sure it is in neutral and the parking brake is on.
If it has an automatic transmission, make sure it is in park.

6 Unlock the steering wheel using a flat blade screwdriver.
Take the screwdriver and place it at the top center of the steering column. Push the screwdriver between the steering wheel and the column. Push the locking pin away from the wheel. Be very firm when pushing the pin; it will not break.

HOW TO PERFORM A FAST 180-DEGREE TURN WITH YOUR CAR

FROM REVERSE

1 Put the car in reverse.

2 Select a spot straight ahead. Keep your eyes on it, and begin backing up.

3 Jam on the gas.

4 Cut the wheel sharply ninety degrees around (a quarter turn) as you simultaneously drop the transmission into drive.

Make sure you have enough speed to use the momentum of the car to swing it around, but remember that going too fast (greater than forty-five miles per hour) can be dangerous and may flip the car (and strip your gears). Turning the wheel left will swing the rear of the car left; turning it right will swing the car right.

5 When the car has completed the turn, step on the gas and head off.

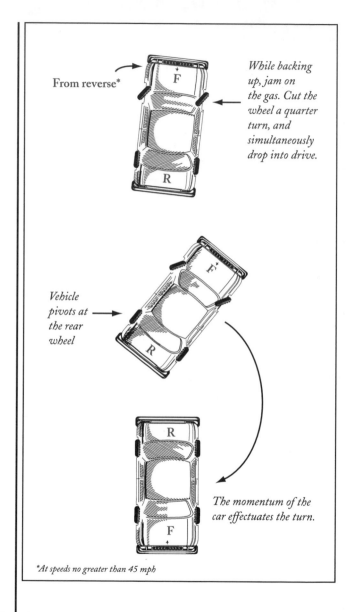

From reverse*

While backing up, jam on the gas. Cut the wheel a quarter turn, and simultaneously drop into drive.

Vehicle pivots at the rear wheel

The momentum of the car effectuates the turn.

*At speeds no greater than 45 mph

FROM DRIVE

1 While in drive, or a forward gear, accelerate to a moderate rate of speed (anything faster than forty-five miles per hour risks flipping the car).

2 Slip the car into neutral to prevent the front wheels from spinning.

3 Take your foot off the gas and turn the wheel ninety degrees (a quarter turn) while pulling hard on the emergency brake.

4 As the rear swings around, return the wheel to its original position and put the car back into drive.

5 Step on the gas to start moving in the direction from which you came.

Be Aware
- The 180-degree turn while moving forward is more difficult for the following reasons:
- It is easier to swing the front of the car around, because it is heavier and it will move faster with momentum.
- It is harder to maintain control of the rear of the car—it is lighter and will slip more easily than the front. Spinning out of control, or flipping the car, are potential dangers.
- Road conditions can play a significant role in the success—and safety—of this maneuver. Any surface without sufficient traction (dirt, mud, ice, gravel) will make quick turns harder and collisions more likely.

performing a fast 180-degree turn with your car

HOW TO
RAM A CAR

Ramming a car to move it out of your way is not easy or safe, but there are some methods that work better than others and some that will minimize the damage to your vehicle. Keep in mind that the best way to hit a car blocking your path is to clip the very rear of it, about one foot from the rear bumper. The rear is the lightest part of a car, and it will move relatively easily. Hitting it in the rear can also disable the car—with the rear wheel crushed, you have time to get away without being pursued.

1 Disable your air bag, if you can.
It will deploy on impact and will obstruct your view after it deploys.

2 Wear a seat belt.

3 Accelerate to at least twenty-five miles per hour.
Do not go too fast—keeping the car at a slow speed will allow you to maintain control without slowing down. Then, just before impact, increase your speed to greater than thirty miles per hour to deliver a disabling crunch to the rear wheel of the obstacle car.

4 Ram the front passenger side of your car into the obstacle car at its rear wheel, at a ninety-degree angle (the cars should be perpendicular).

5 If you are unable to hit a car in the rear, go for the front corner.
Avoid hitting the car squarely in the side; this will not move it out of your way.

6 The car should spin out of your way—hit the gas, and keep moving.

Ram the obstacle car with the passenger side of your car, and deliver a disabling crunch to its rear wheel.

If you are unable to hit the car in the rear, go for the right corner.

HOW TO
ESCAPE FROM
A SINKING CAR

1 As soon as you hit the water, open your window.
This is your best chance of escape, because opening
the door will be very difficult given the outside water
pressure. (To be safe, you should drive with the windows and doors slightly open whenever you are near
water or are driving on ice.) Opening the windows
allows water to come in and equalize the pressure.
Once the water pressure inside and outside the car is
equal, you'll be able to open the door.

2 If your power windows won't work or you cannot
roll your windows down all the way, attempt to
break the glass with your foot or shoulder or a heavy
object such as an antitheft steering wheel lock.

3 Get out.
Do not worry about leaving anything behind unless it
is another person. Vehicles with engines in front will
sink at a steep angle. If the water is fifteen feet or
deeper, the vehicle may end up on its roof, upside
down. For this reason, you must get out as soon as
possible, while the car is still afloat. Depending on the
vehicle, floating time will range from a few seconds to
a few minutes. The more airtight the car, the longer it
floats. Air in the car will quickly be forced out

As soon as you hit the water open your window. Otherwise, the pressure of the water will make it very difficult to escape.

If you were unable to exit before hitting the water, attempt to break a window with your foot or a heavy object.

through the trunk and cab, and an air bubble is unlikely to remain once the car hits bottom. Get out as early as possible.

4 If you are unable to open the window or break it, you have one final option.
Remain calm and do not panic. Wait until the car begins filling with water. When the water reaches your

head, take a deep breath and hold it. Now the pressure should be equalized inside and outside, and you should be able to open the door and swim to the surface.

How to Avoid Breaking through the Ice

- Cars and light trucks need at least eight inches of clear, solid ice on which to drive safely.
- Driving early or late in the season is not advisable.
- Leaving your car in one place for a long period of time can weaken the ice beneath it, and cars should not be parked—or driven—close together.
- Cross any cracks at right angles, and drive slowly.
- New ice is generally thicker than old ice.
- Direct freezing of lake or stream water is stronger than refreezing, freezing of melting snow, or freezing of water bubbling up through cracks.
- If there is a layer of snow on the ice, beware: a layer of snow insulates the ice, slowing the freezing process, and the snow's weight can decrease the bearing capacity of the ice.
- Ice near the shore is weaker.
- River ice is generally weaker than lake ice.
- River mouths are dangerous, because the ice near them is weaker.
- Carry several large nails in your pocket, and a length of rope. The nails will help you pull yourself out of the ice, and the rope can be thrown to someone on more solid ice, or can be used to help someone else.

HOW TO DEAL WITH A DOWNED POWER LINE

High-voltage power lines, which carry power from plants and transformers to customers, can come crashing down during severe storms. If you are in a car when a pole or line falls, you are much safer remaining inside a grounded vehicle than being on foot. If the wire falls on the car, do not touch anything—wait for help.

1 Assume that all power lines, whether sparking or not, are live.

2 Stay far away from downed lines.
Current can travel through any conductive material, and water on the ground can provide a "channel" from the power line to you. An electrical shock can also occur when one comes in contact with the charged particles near a high-voltage line; direct contact is not necessary for electrocution to occur. Never touch a vehicle that has come in contact with a live wire—it may still retain a charge.

3 Do not assume that a nonsparking wire is safe.
Often, power may be restored by automated equipment, causing a "dead" wire to become dangerous. Stay away from downed lines even if you know they are not electric lines—the line could have come in contact with an electric line when it fell, causing the downed line to be "hot."

4 If a person comes into contact with a live wire, use a nonconductive material to separate the person from the electrical source.

Use a wooden broom handle, a wooden chair, or a dry towel or sheet. Rubber or insulated gloves offer no protection.

5 Avoid direct contact with the skin of the victim or any conducting material touching it until he or she is disconnected; you may be shocked also.

6 Check the pulse and begin rescue breathing and CPR if necessary.

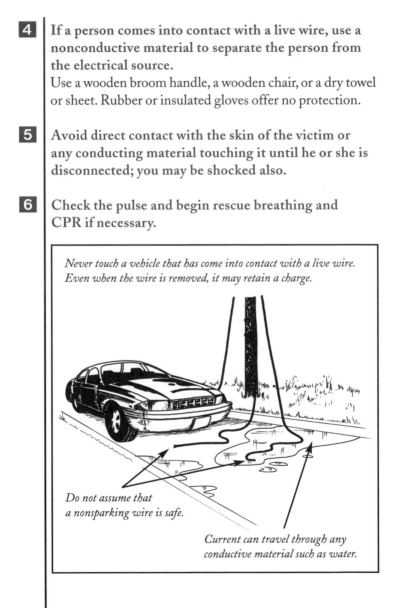

Never touch a vehicle that has come into contact with a live wire. Even when the wire is removed, it may retain a charge.

Do not assume that a nonsparking wire is safe.

Current can travel through any conductive material such as water.

CHAPTER 2
THE BEST DEFENSE

HOW TO SURVIVE A POISONOUS SNAKE ATTACK

Because poisonous snakes can be difficult to identify—and because some nonpoisonous snakes have markings very similar to venomous ones—the best way to avoid getting bitten is to leave all snakes alone. Assume that a snake is venomous unless you know for certain that it is not.

How to Treat a Bite

1 Wash the bite with soap and water as soon as you can.

2 Immobilize the bitten area and keep it lower than the heart.
This will slow the flow of the venom.

3 Get medical help as soon as possible.
A doctor should treat all snakebites unless you are willing to bet your life that the offending snake is nonpoisonous. Of about eight thousand venomous bites a year in the U.S., nine to fifteen victims are killed. A bite from any type of poisonous snake should always be considered a medical emergency. Even bites from nonpoisonous snakes should be treated professionally, as severe allergic reactions can occur. Some

Mojave rattlesnakes carry a neurotoxic venom that can affect the brain or spinal cord, causing paralysis.

4 Immediately wrap a bandage tightly two to four inches above the bite to help slow the venom if you are unable to reach medical care within thirty minutes. The bandage should not cut off blood flow from a vein or artery. Make the bandage loose enough for a finger to slip underneath.

5 If you have a first aid kit equipped with a suction device, follow the instructions for helping to draw venom out of the wound without making an incision. Generally, you will need to place the rubber suction cup over the wound and attempt to draw the venom out from the bite marks.

WHAT NOT TO DO

- Do not place any ice or cooling element on the bite; this will make removing the venom with suction more difficult.
- Do not tie a bandage or a tourniquet too tightly. If used incorrectly, a tourniquet can cut blood flow completely and damage the limb.
- Do not make any incision on or around the wound in an attempt to remove the venom—there is danger of infection.
- Do not attempt to suck out the venom. You do not want it in your mouth, where it might enter your bloodstream.

Snakes coil before they strike.

Snakes can strike at a distance approximately half their length; half their body does not leave the ground.

How to Escape from a Python

Unlike poisonous snakes, pythons and boas kill their prey not through the injection of venom but by constriction; hence these snakes are known as constrictors. A constrictor coils its body around its prey, squeezing it until the pressure is great enough to kill.

Since pythons and boas can grow to be nearly twenty feet long, they are fully capable of killing a grown person, and small children are even more vulnerable. The good news is that most pythons will strike and then try to get away, rather than consume a full-grown human.

1 Remain still.
This will minimize constriction strength, but a python usually continues constricting well after the prey is dead and not moving.

2 Try to control the python's head and try to unwrap the coils, starting from whichever end is available.

How to Avoid an Attack

- Do not try to get a closer look, prod the snake to make it move, or try to kill it.
- If you come across a snake, back away slowly and give it a wide berth: snakes can easily strike half their body length in an instant, and some species are six feet or longer.
- When hiking in an area with poisonous snakes, always wear thick leather boots and long pants.
- Keep to marked trails.
- Snakes are cold-blooded and need the sun to help regulate their body temperature. They are often found lying on warm rocks or in other sunny places.

HOW TO FEND OFF A SHARK

1 Hit back.
If a shark is coming toward you or attacks you, use anything you have in your possession—a camera, probe, harpoon gun, your fist—to hit the shark's eyes or gills, which are the areas most sensitive to pain.

2 Make quick, sharp, repeated jabs in these areas.
Sharks are predators and will usually only follow through on an attack if they have the advantage, so making the shark unsure of its advantage in any way possible will increase your chances of survival. Contrary to popular opinion, the shark's nose is not the area to attack, unless you cannot reach the eyes or gills. Hitting the shark simply tells it that you are not defenseless.

HOW TO AVOID AN ATTACK

- Always stay in groups—sharks are more likely to attack an individual.
- Do not wander too far from shore. This isolates you and creates the additional danger of being too far from assistance.
- Avoid being in the water during darkness or twilight hours, when sharks are most active and have a competitive sensory advantage.

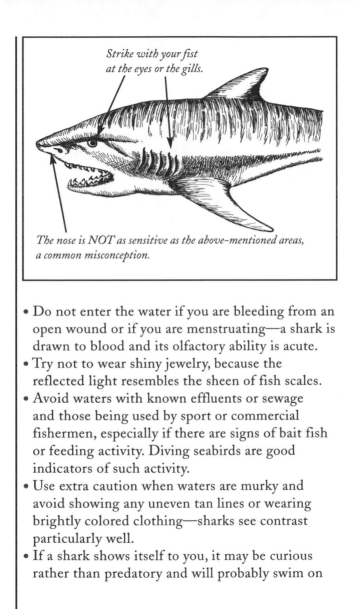

Strike with your fist at the eyes or the gills.

The nose is NOT as sensitive as the above-mentioned areas, a common misconception.

- Do not enter the water if you are bleeding from an open wound or if you are menstruating—a shark is drawn to blood and its olfactory ability is acute.
- Try not to wear shiny jewelry, because the reflected light resembles the sheen of fish scales.
- Avoid waters with known effluents or sewage and those being used by sport or commercial fishermen, especially if there are signs of bait fish or feeding activity. Diving seabirds are good indicators of such activity.
- Use extra caution when waters are murky and avoid showing any uneven tan lines or wearing brightly colored clothing—sharks see contrast particularly well.
- If a shark shows itself to you, it may be curious rather than predatory and will probably swim on

and leave you alone. If you are under the surface and lucky enough to see an attacking shark, then you do have a good chance of defending yourself if the shark is not too large.

- Scuba divers should avoid lying on the surface, where they may look like a piece of prey to a shark, and from where they cannot see a shark approaching.
- A shark attack is a potential danger for anyone who frequents marine waters, but it should be kept in perspective. Bees, wasps, and snakes are responsible for far more fatalities each year, and in the United States the annual risk of death from lightning is thirty times greater than from a shark attack.

THREE KINDS OF SHARK ATTACKS

"HIT AND RUN" ATTACKS are by far the most common. These typically occur in the surf zone, where swimmers and surfers are the targets. The victim seldom sees its attacker, and the shark does not return after inflicting a single bite or slash wound.

"BUMP AND BITE" ATTACKS are characterized by the shark initially circling and often bumping the victim prior to the actual attack. These types of attacks usually involve divers or swimmers in deeper waters, but also occur in nearshore shallows in some areas of the world.

"SNEAK" ATTACKS differ: the strike can occur without warning. With both "bump and bite" and "sneak" attacks, repeat attacks are common and multiple and sustained bites are the norm. Injuries incurred during this type of attack are usually quite severe, frequently resulting in death.

Be Aware

Most shark attacks occur in nearshore waters, typically inshore of a sandbar or between sandbars where sharks feed and can become trapped at low tide. Areas with steep drop-offs are also likely attack sites. Sharks congregate in these areas, because their natural prey congregates there. Almost any large shark, roughly six feet or longer in total length, is a potential threat to humans. But three species in particular have repeatedly attacked man: the white shark *(Carcharodon carcharias)*, the tiger shark *(Galeocerdo cuvieri)*, and the bull shark *(Carcharhinus leucas)*. All are cosmopolitan in distribution, reach large sizes, and consume large prey such as marine mammals, sea turtles, and fish as normal elements of their diets.

HOW TO ESCAPE FROM A BEAR

1 Lie still and quiet.
Documented attacks show that an attack by a mother black bear often ends when the person stops fighting.

2 Stay where you are and do not climb a tree to escape a bear.
Black bears can climb trees quickly and easily and will come after you. The odds are that the bear will leave you alone if you stay put.

3 If you are lying still and the bear attacks, strike back with anything you can.
Go for the bear's eyes or its snout.

What to Do If You See a Bear

- Make your presence known by talking loudly, clapping, singing, or occasionally calling out. (Some people prefer to wear bells.) Whatever you do, be heard—it does not pay to surprise a bear. Remember, bears can run much faster than humans.
- Keep children close at hand and within sight.
- There is no guaranteed minimum safe distance from a bear: the farther, the better.
- If you are in a car, remain in your vehicle. Do not get out, even for a quick photo. Keep your windows up. Do not impede the bear from crossing the road.

While all bears are dangerous, these three situations render even more of a threat.

Females protecting cubs

Bears habituated to human food.

Bears defending a fresh kill.

How to Avoid an Attack

- Reduce or eliminate food odors from yourself, your camp, your clothes, and your vehicle.
- Do not sleep in the same clothes you cook in.
- Store food so that bears cannot smell or reach it.
- Do not keep food in your tent—not even a chocolate bar.
- Properly store and bring out all garbage.
- Handle and store pet food with as much care as your own.
- While all bears should be considered dangerous and should be avoided, three types should be regarded as more dangerous than the average bear. These are:

  > Females defending cubs.
  > Bears habituated to human food.
  > Bears defending a fresh kill.

Be Aware

There are about 650,000 black bears in North America, and only one person every three years is killed by a bear—although there are hundreds of thousands of encounters. Most bears in the continental U.S. are black bears, but black bears are not always black in color: sometimes their fur is brown or blond. Males are generally bigger than females (125 to 500 pounds for males, 90 to 300 pounds for females).

- Bears can run as fast as horses, uphill or downhill.
- Bears can climb trees, although black bears are better tree-climbers than grizzly bears.
- Bears have excellent senses of smell and hearing.
- Bears are extremely strong. They can tear cars apart looking for food.
- Every bear defends a "personal space." The extent of this space will vary with each bear and each situation; it may be a few meters or a few hundred meters. Intrusion into this space is considered a threat and may provoke an attack.
- Bears aggressively defend their food.
- All female bears defend their cubs. If a female with cubs is surprised at close range or is separated from her cubs, she may attack.
- An aggressive reaction to any danger to her cubs is the mother grizzly's natural defense.
- A female black bear's natural defense is to chase her cubs up a tree and defend them from the base.
- Stay away from dead animals. Bears may attack to defend such food.
- It is best not to hike with dogs, as dogs can antagonize bears and cause an attack. An unleashed dog may even bring a bear back to you.

HOW TO
ESCAPE FROM
A MOUNTAIN LION

1 Do not run.
The animal most likely will have seen and smelled
you already, and running will simply cause it to pay
more attention.

2 Try to make yourself appear bigger by opening
your coat wide.
The mountain lion is less likely to attack a larger
animal.

3 Do not crouch down.
Hold your ground, wave your hands, and shout. Show
it that you are not defenseless.

4 If you have small children with you, pick them up—
do all you can to appear larger.
Children, who move quickly and have high-pitched
voices, are at higher risk than adults.

5 Back away slowly or wait until the animal
moves away.
Report any lion sightings to authorities as soon as
possible.

Upon sighting a mountain lion, do not run.
Do not crouch down. Try to make yourself appear
larger by opening wide your coat.

6 If the lion still behaves aggressively, throw stones. Convince the lion that you are not prey and that you may be dangerous yourself.

7 Fight back if you are attacked.
Most mountain lions are small enough that an average size human will be able to ward off an attack by fighting back aggressively. Hit the mountain lion in the head, especially around the eyes and mouth. Use sticks, fists, or whatever is at hand. Do not curl up and play dead. Mountain lions generally leap down upon prey from above and deliver a "killing bite" to the back of the neck. Their technique is to break the neck and knock down the prey, and they also will rush and lunge up at the neck of prey, dragging the victim down while holding the neck in a crushing grip. Protect your neck and throat at all costs.

How to Avoid an Attack

Mountain lions, also called cougars, have been known to attack people without provocation; aggressive ones have attacked hikers and especially small children, resulting in serious injury. Still, most mountain lions will avoid people. To minimize your contact with cougars in an area inhabited by them, avoid hiking alone and at dusk and dawn, when mountain lions are more active.

HOW TO WRESTLE FREE FROM AN ALLIGATOR

1 If you are on land, try to get on the alligator's back and put downward pressure on its neck.
This will force its head and jaws down.

2 Cover the alligator's eyes.
This will usually make it more sedate.

3 If you are attacked, go for the eyes and nose.
Use any weapon you have, or your fist.

4 If its jaws are closed on something you want to remove (for example, a limb), tap or punch it on the snout.
Alligators often open their mouths when tapped lightly. They may drop whatever it is they have taken hold of, and back off.

5 If the alligator gets you in its jaws, you must prevent it from shaking you or from rolling over—these instinctual actions cause severe tissue damage.
Try to keep the mouth clamped shut so the alligator does not begin shaking.

6 Seek medical attention immediately, even for a small cut or bruise, to treat infection.
Alligators have a huge number of pathogens in their mouths.

wrestling free from an alligator

To get an alligator to release something it has in its mouth, tap it on the snout.

How to Avoid an Attack

While deaths in the United States from alligator attacks are rare, there are thousands of attacks and hundreds of fatalities from Nile crocodiles in Africa and Indopacific crocodiles in Asia and Australia. A few tips to keep in mind:

- Do not swim or wade in areas alligators are known to inhabit (in Florida, this can be anywhere).
- Do not swim or wade alone, and always check out the area before venturing in.
- Never feed alligators.
- Do not dangle arms and legs from boats, and avoid throwing unused bait or fish from a boat or dock.

- Do not harass, try to touch, or capture any alligator.
- Leave babies and eggs alone. Any adult alligator will respond to a distress call from any youngster. Mother alligators guarding nests and babies will defend them.
- In most cases the attacking alligators had been fed by humans prior to the attack. This is an important link—feeding alligators seems to cause them to lose their fear of humans and become more aggressive.

HOW TO ESCAPE
FROM KILLER BEES

1 | If bees begin flying around and/or stinging you, do not freeze.
Run away; swatting at the bees only makes them angrier.

2 | Get indoors as fast as you can.

3 | If no shelter is available, run through bushes or high weeds.
This will help give you cover.

4 | If a bee stings you, it will leave its stinger in your skin.
Remove the stinger by raking your fingernail across it in a sideways motion. Do not pinch or pull the stinger out—this may squeeze more venom from the stinger into your body. Do not let stingers remain in the skin, because venom can continue to pump into the body for up to ten minutes.

5 | Do not jump into a swimming pool or other body of water—the bees are likely to be waiting for you when you surface.

If bees begin flying around and /or stinging you,
DO NOT freeze; DO NOT swat them. Run away.
If no shelter is available, run through bushes or high weeds.

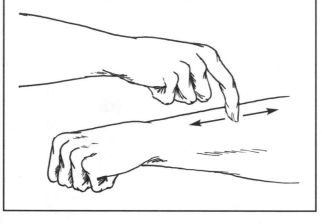

If a bee stings you, remove the stinger by raking your fingernail across it in a sideways motion. Do not pinch the area.

RISK OF ATTACK

The Africanized honeybee is a cousin of the run-of-the-mill domesticated honeybee that has lived in the United States for centuries. The "killer bee" moniker was created after some magazine reports about several deaths that resulted from Africanized bee stings some years back. Africanized honeybees are considered "wild;" they are easily angered by animals and people, and likely to become aggressive.

Bees "swarm" most often in the spring and fall. This is when the entire colony moves to establish a new hive. They may move in large masses—called swarms—until they find a suitable spot. Once the colony is built and the bees begin raising their young, they will protect their hive by stinging.

While any colony of bees will defend its hive, Africanized bees do so with gusto. These bees can kill, and they present a danger even to those who are not allergic to bee stings. In several isolated instances, people and animals have been stung to death. Regular honeybees will chase you about fifty yards. Africanized honeybees may pursue you three times that distance.

Most often, death from stings occurs when people are not able to get away from the bees quickly. Animal losses have occurred for the same reasons—pets and livestock were tied up or penned when they encountered the bees and could not escape.

To Minimize Risk

- Avoid colonies by filling in holes or cracks in exterior walls, filling in tree cavities, and putting screens on the tops of rainspouts and over water meter boxes in the ground.
- Do not bother bee colonies: if you see that bees are building—or have already built—a colony around your home, do not disturb them. Call a pest control center to find out who removes bees.

HOW TO
DEAL WITH A
CHARGING BULL

1 Do not antagonize the bull, and do not move.
Bulls will generally leave humans alone unless they
become angry.

2 Look around for a safe haven—an escape route,
cover, or high ground.
Running away is not likely to help unless you find an
open door, a fence to jump, or another safe haven—
bulls can easily outrun humans. If you can reach a safe
spot, make a run for it.

3 If a safe haven is not available, remove your shirt,
hat, or another article of clothing.
Use this to distract the bull. It does not matter what
color the clothing is. Despite the colors bullfighters
traditionally use, bulls do not naturally head for red—
they react to and move toward movement, not color.

4 If the bull charges, remain still and then throw your
shirt or hat away from you.
The bull should head toward the object you've thrown.

If you cannot find safe cover from a charging bull, remove articles of clothing and throw them away from your body. The bull will veer and head toward the moving objects.

IF YOU ENCOUNTER A STAMPEDE

If you encounter a stampede of bulls or cattle, do not try to distract them. Try to determine where they are headed, and then get out of the way. If you cannot escape, your only option is to run alongside the stampede to avoid getting trampled. Bulls are not like horses, and will not avoid you if you lie down—so keep moving.

HOW TO WIN
A SWORD FIGHT

Always keep your sword in the "ready" position—held in front of you, with both hands, and perpendicular to the ground. With this method, you can move the sword side to side and up and down easily, blocking and landing blows in all directions by moving your arms. Hold the tip of the sword at a bit of an angle, with the tip pointed slightly toward your opponent. Picture a doorway—you should be able to move your sword in any direction and quickly hit any edge of the doorframe.

How to Deflect and Counter a Blow

1 Step up and into the blow, with your arms held against your body.
React quickly and against your instincts, which will tell you to move back and away. By moving closer, you can cut off a blow's power. Avoid extending your arms, which would make your own counterblow less powerful.

2 Push or "punch" at the blow instead of simply trying to absorb it with your own sword.
If a blow is aimed at your head, move your sword completely parallel to the ground and above your head. Block with the center of your sword, not the end. Always move out toward your opponent, even if you are defending and not attacking.

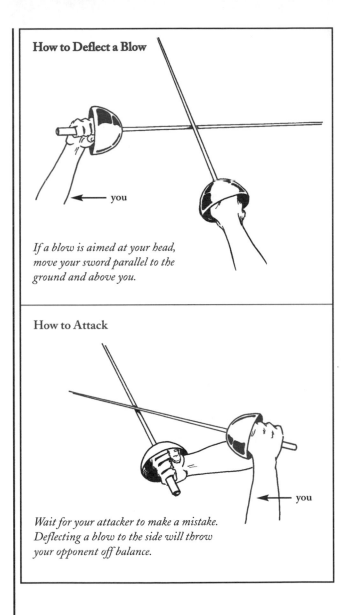

How to Deflect a Blow

← you

If a blow is aimed at your head, move your sword parallel to the ground and above you.

How to Attack

← you

Wait for your attacker to make a mistake. Deflecting a blow to the side will throw your opponent off balance.

How to Attack

1 | Move the sword in steady, quick blows up and down and to the left and right.
Assuming you must disable your attacker, do not try to stab with your sword. A stabbing motion will put you off balance and will leave your sword far out in front of you, making you vulnerable to a counterblow.

2 | Do not raise the sword up behind your head to try a huge blow—you will end up with a sword in your gut.

3 | Hold your position, punch out to defend, and strike quickly.

4 | Wait for your attacker to make a mistake.
Stepping into a blow or deflecting it to the side will put him/her off balance. Once your opponent is off balance, you can take advantage of their moment of weakness by landing a disabling blow, remembering not to jab with your sword but to strike up and down or from side to side.

HOW TO
TAKE A PUNCH

A BLOW TO THE BODY

1 Tighten your stomach muscles.
A body blow to the gut (solar plexus) can damage organs and kill. This sort of punch is one of the best and easiest ways to knock someone out. (Harry Houdini died from an unexpected blow to the abdomen.)

2 Do not suck in your stomach if you expect that a punch is imminent.

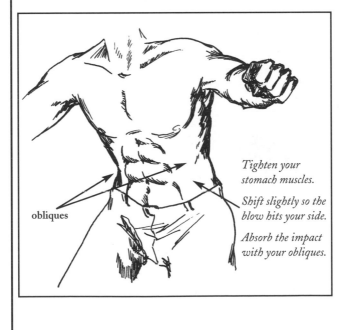

obliques

Tighten your stomach muscles.

Shift slightly so the blow hits your side.

Absorb the impact with your obliques.

3 If possible, shift slightly so that the blow hits your side, but do not flinch or move away from the punch. Try to absorb the blow with your obliques: this is the set of muscles on your side that wraps around your ribs. While a blow to this area may crack a rib, it is less likely to do damage to internal organs.

A Blow to the Head

1 Move toward the blow, not away from it.
Getting punched while moving backward will result in the head taking the punch at full force. A punch to the face can cause head whipping, where the brain moves suddenly inside the skull, and may result in severe injury or death.

2 Tighten your neck muscles and clench your jaw to avoid scraping of the upper and lower palettes.

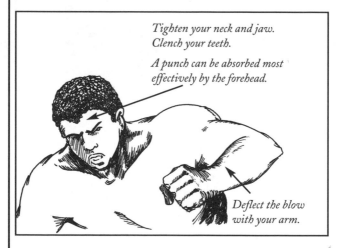

Tighten your neck and jaw. Clench your teeth.

A punch can be absorbed most effectively by the forehead.

Deflect the blow with your arm.

A Straight Punch

1 The straight punch—one that comes straight at your face—should be countered by moving toward the blow.
This will take force from the blow.

2 A punch can be absorbed most effectively and with the least injury by the forehead.
Avoid taking the punch in the nose, which is extremely painful.

3 Attempt to deflect the blow with an arm.
Moving into the punch may result in your attacker missing the mark wide to either side.

4 (optional) Hit back with an uppercut or roundhouse.

A Roundhouse Punch

1 Clench your jaw.
A punch to the ear causes great pain and can break your jaw.

2 Move in close to your attacker.
Try to make the punch land harmlessly behind your head.

3 (optional) Hit back with an uppercut.

taking a punch

An Uppercut

1 Clench your neck and jaw.
An uppercut can cause much damage, whipping your head back, easily breaking your jaw or your nose.

2 Use your arm to absorb some of the impact or deflect the blow to the side—anything to minimize the impact of a straight punch to the jaw.

3 Do not step into this punch.
If possible, move your head to the side.

4 (optional) Hit back with a straight punch to the face or with an uppercut of your own.

LEAPS OF FAITH

HOW TO JUMP FROM A BRIDGE OR CLIFF INTO A RIVER

When attempting a high fall (over twenty feet) into water in an emergency situation, you will not know much about your surroundings, specifically the depth of the water. This makes jumping particularly dangerous.

If jumping from a bridge into a river or other body of water with boat traffic, try to land in the channel—the deepwater area where boats go under the bridge. This area is generally in the center, away from the shoreline.

Stay away from any area with pylons that are supporting the bridge. Debris can collect in these areas and you can hit it when you enter the water.

Swim to shore immediately after surfacing.

How to Jump

1 Jump feet first.

2 Keep your body completely vertical.

3 Squeeze your feet together.

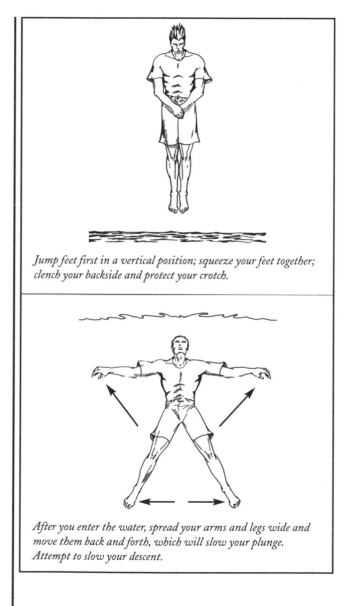

Jump feet first in a vertical position; squeeze your feet together; clench your backside and protect your crotch.

After you enter the water, spread your arms and legs wide and move them back and forth, which will slow your plunge. Attempt to slow your descent.

jumping from a bridge or cliff into a river

4 Enter the water feet first, and clench your buttocks together.

If you do not, water may rush in and cause severe internal damage.

5 Protect your crotch area by covering it with your hands.

6 Immediately after you hit the water, spread your arms and legs wide and move them back and forth to generate resistance, which will slow your plunge to the bottom.

Always assume the water is not deep enough to keep you from hitting bottom.

Be Aware

• Hitting the water as described above could save your life, although it may break your legs.

• If your body is not straight, you can break your back upon entry. Keep yourself vertical until you hit the water.

• Do not even think about going in headfirst unless you are absolutely sure that the water is at least twenty feet deep. If your legs hit the bottom, they will break. If your head hits, your skull will break.

HOW TO JUMP FROM A BUILDING INTO A DUMPSTER

How to Jump

1 Jump straight down.
If you leap off and away from the building at an angle, your trajectory will make you miss the Dumpster. Resist your natural tendency to push off.

2 Tuck your head and bring your legs around.
To do this during the fall, execute a three-quarter revolution—basically, a not-quite-full somersault. This is the only method that will allow a proper landing, with your back facing down.

3 Aim for the center of the Dumpster or large box of debris.

4 Land flat on your back so that when your body folds, your feet and hands meet.
When your body hits any surface from a significant height, the body folds into a V. This means landing on your stomach can result in a broken back.

1. Jump straight down.

2. Tuck your head and bring your legs around, executing a three-quarter somersault.

3. Aim for the center of the Dumpster and land flat on your back.

Be Aware

- If the building has fire escapes or other protrusions, your leap will have to be far enough out so you miss them on your way down. The landing target needs to be far enough from the building for you to hit it.
- The Dumpster may be filled with bricks or other unfriendly materials. It is entirely possible to survive a high fall (five stories or more) into a Dumpster, provided it is filled with the right type of trash (cardboard boxes are best) and you land correctly.

HOW TO MANEUVER ON TOP OF A MOVING TRAIN AND GET INSIDE

1   Do not try to stand up straight (you probably will not be able to anyway).

Stay bent slightly forward, leaning into the wind. If the train is moving faster than thirty miles per hour, it will be difficult to maintain your balance and resist the wind, so crawling on all fours may be the best method until you can get down.

2   If the train is approaching a turn, lie flat; do not try to keep your footing.

The car may have guide rails along the edge to direct water. If it does, grab them and hold on.

3   If the train is approaching a tunnel entrance, lie flat, and quickly.

There is actually quite a bit of clearance between the top of the train and the top of the tunnel—about three feet—but not nearly enough room to stand. Do not assume that you can walk or crawl to the end of the car to get down and inside before you reach the tunnel—you probably won't.

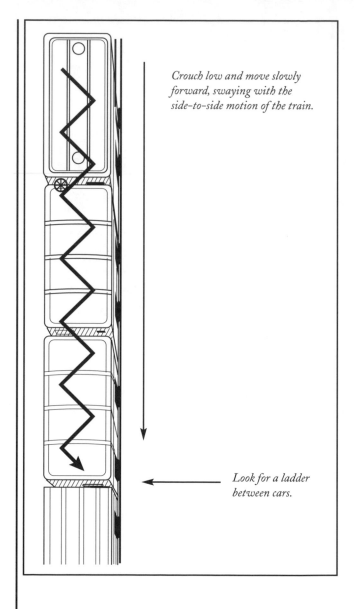

Crouch low and move slowly forward, swaying with the side-to-side motion of the train.

Look for a ladder between cars.

chapter 3: leaps of faith

4 Move your body with the rhythm of the train—from side to side and forward.

Do not proceed in a straight line. Spread your feet apart about thirty-six inches and wobble from side to side as you move forward.

5 Find the ladder at the end of the car (between two cars) and climb down.

It is very unlikely that there will be a ladder on the side of the car—they usually appear only in the movies, to make the stunts more exciting.

Be Aware

The sizes and shapes of the cars on a freight train may vary widely. This can either make it easier or significantly more difficult to cross from one car to another. A twelve-foot-high boxcar may be next to a flatbed or a rounded chem car. If on this type of train, your best bet is to get down as quickly as possible, rather than to try a dangerous leap from car to car.

HOW TO JUMP FROM A MOVING CAR

Hurling yourself from a moving car should be a last resort, for example if your brakes are defective and your car is about to head off a cliff or into a train.

1 Apply the emergency brake.
This may not stop the car, but it might slow it down enough to make jumping safer.

2 Open the car door.

3 Make sure you jump at an angle that will take you out of the path of the car.
Since your body will be moving at the same velocity as the car, you're going to continue to move in the direction the car is moving. If the car is going straight, try to jump at an angle that will take you away from it.

4 Tuck in your head and your arms and legs.

5 Aim for a soft landing site: grass, brush, wood chips, anything but pavement—or a tree.
Stuntpeople wear pads and land in sandpits. You won't have this luxury, but anything that gives a bit when the body hits it will minimize injury.

6 Roll when you hit the ground.

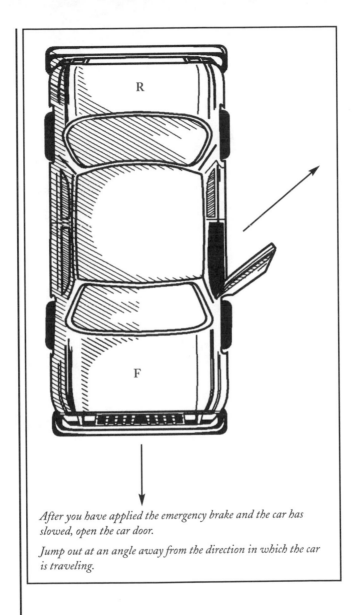

After you have applied the emergency brake and the car has slowed, open the car door.

Jump out at an angle away from the direction in which the car is traveling.

HOW TO LEAP FROM A MOTORCYCLE TO A CAR

If you are planning to enter the car through one of its windows, remember that in many newer cars, only the front windows roll all the way down. You should attempt to be on the front passenger side.

1 Wear a high-quality helmet and a leather jacket plus leather pants and boots.

2 Make sure both vehicles are moving at the same speed.
The slower the speed, the safer the move. Anything faster than sixty miles per hour is extremely dangerous.

3 Wait for a long straight section of road.

4 Get the vehicles as close as possible to each other.
You will be on the passenger side of the car, so you will be very close to the edge of the roadway. Be careful not to swerve.

5 Stand crouched with both of your feet on either the running board or the seat.

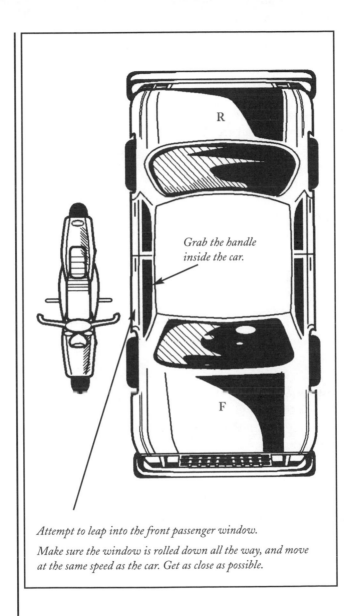

Grab the handle inside the car.

Attempt to leap into the front passenger window.

Make sure the window is rolled down all the way, and move at the same speed as the car. Get as close as possible.

6 | Hold the throttle until the last instant.
Remember, as soon as you release the throttle the bike speed will decrease.

7 | If the car has a handle inside (above the door) grab it with your free hand.
If not, simply time the leap so your torso lands in the car. If someone can grab you and pull you in, all the better.

8 | Have the driver swerve away from the bike as soon as you are inside.
Once you have released the handlebars, the bike will go out of control and crash. It may also slip under the rear passenger-side wheel of the car.

9 | If you miss the window, tuck and roll away from the vehicles (see page 82 for jumping from a moving car).

Be Aware
The move is much easier if two people are on the motorcycle so that the non-jumper can continue driving.

In the movies and in stunt shows, these transfers are usually performed at slow speeds, and in fact often employ the use of a metal step installed on one side of the bike or car, which allows the rider to step off while keeping the bike balanced. You are not likely to have this option.

EMERGENCIES

HOW TO PERFORM A TRACHEOTOMY

This procedure, technically called a cricothyroid-otomy, should be undertaken only when a person with a throat obstruction is not able to breathe at all—no gasping sounds, no coughing—and only after you have attempted to perform the Heimlich maneuver three times without dislodging the obstruction. If possible, someone should call for paramedics while you proceed.

WHAT YOU WILL NEED

- A first aid kit, if available
- A razor blade or very sharp knife
- A straw (two would be better) or a ballpoint pen with the inside (ink-filled tube) removed. If neither a straw nor a pen is available, use stiff paper or cardboard rolled into a tube. Good first aid kits may contain "trache" tubes.

There will not be time for sterilization of your tools, so do not bother; infection is the least of your worries at this point.

chapter 4: emergencies

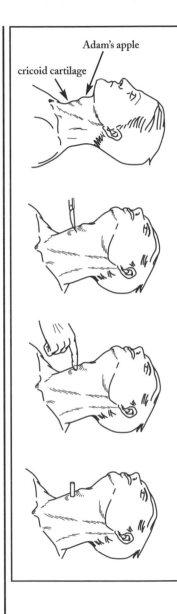

Adam's apple

cricoid cartilage

Find the indentation between the Adam's apple and the cricoid cartilage.

Make a half-inch horizontal incision about one half inch deep.

Pinch the incision or insert your finger inside the slit to open it.

Insert your tube into the incision, roughly one-half to one inch deep.

performing a tracheotomy

How to Proceed

1 Find the person's Adam's apple (thyroid cartilage).

2 Move your finger about one inch down the neck until you feel another bulge.
This is the cricoid cartilage. The indentation between the two is the cricothyroid membrane, where the incision will be made.

3 Take the razor blade or knife and make a half-inch horizontal incision.
The cut should be about half an inch deep. There should not be too much blood.

4 Pinch the incision open or place your finger inside the slit to open it.

5 Insert your tube in the incision, roughly one-half to one inch deep.

6 Breathe into the tube with two quick breaths.
Pause five seconds, then give one breath every five seconds.

7 You will see the chest rise and the person should regain consciousness if you have performed the procedure correctly.
The person should be able to breathe on their own, albeit with some difficulty, until help arrives.

HOW TO USE A DEFIBRILLATOR TO RESTORE A HEARTBEAT

Defibrillation is the delivery of a powerful electrical shock to the heart. (The defibrillator is the device used in movies and TV shows: two handheld pads are placed on the victim's chest while an actor yells "Clear!") In the past, defibrillators were very heavy, expensive, needed regular maintenance, and were mostly found only in hospitals. Now there are more portable units available. A defibrillator should be used only for a Sudden Cardiac Arrest (SCA), an electrical problem that cannot be helped by CPR.

How to Use a Defibrillator

1 Turn on the defibrillator by pressing the green button. Most machines will provide both visual and voice prompts.

2 First, remove the person's shirt and jewelry, then apply the pads to the chest as shown in the diagram displayed on the machine's LED panel.
One pad should be placed on the upper right side of the chest, one on the lower left.

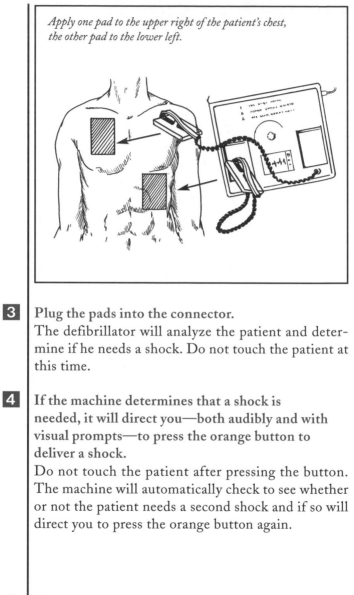

*Apply one pad to the upper right of the patient's chest,
the other pad to the lower left.*

3 Plug the pads into the connector.
The defibrillator will analyze the patient and determine if he needs a shock. Do not touch the patient at
this time.

4 If the machine determines that a shock is
needed, it will direct you—both audibly and with
visual prompts—to press the orange button to
deliver a shock.
Do not touch the patient after pressing the button.
The machine will automatically check to see whether
or not the patient needs a second shock and if so will
direct you to press the orange button again.

5 Check the patient's airway, breathing, and pulse. If there is a pulse but the patient is not breathing, begin mouth-to-mouth resuscitation. If there is no pulse, repeat the defibrillation process.

Be Aware
A defibrillator should be used for a person experiencing sudden cardiac arrest (SCA), a condition where the heart's electrical signals become confused and the heart ceases to function. A person experiencing SCA will stop breathing, the pulse will slow or stop, and consciousness will be lost.

HOW TO
IDENTIFY A BOMB

Letter and package bombs can be very dangerous and destructive. However, unlike a bomb that goes off suddenly and with no warning, they can be identified. Observe the following procedures and warning signs.

HOW TO DETECT A LETTER BOMB

1 If a carrier delivers an unexpected bulky letter or parcel, inspect it for lumps, bulges, or protrusions, without applying pressure.
Check for unevenly balanced parcels.

2 Handwritten addresses or labels from companies are unusual.
Check to see if the company exists and if they sent a package or letter.

3 Be suspicious of packages wrapped in string—modern packaging materials have eliminated the need for twine or string.

4 Watch out for excess postage on small packages or letters—this indicates that the object was not weighed by the post office.
It is no longer legal to mail stamped parcels weighing more than sixteen ounces at mailboxes in the United States—they must be taken to a post office.

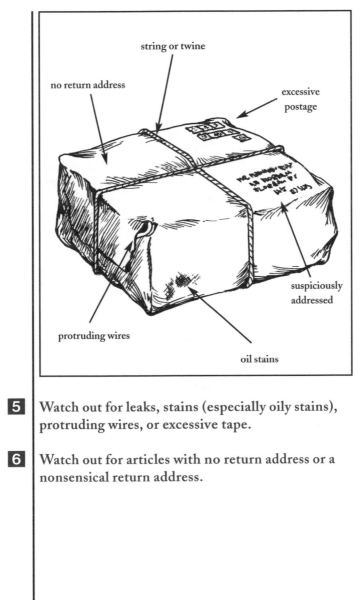

string or twine

no return address

excessive postage

suspiciously addressed

protruding wires

oil stains

5 | Watch out for leaks, stains (especially oily stains), protruding wires, or excessive tape.

6 | Watch out for articles with no return address or a nonsensical return address.

How to Search for a Bomb

Government agencies use well-defined search procedures for bombs and explosive devices. After a bomb threat, the following can be used as a guide for searching a room, using a two-person search team.

1 Divide the area and select a search height.
The first searching sweep should cover all items resting on the floor up to the height of furniture; subsequent sweeps should move up from there.

2 Start back-to-back and work around the room, in opposite directions, moving toward each other.

3 Search around the walls and proceed inward in concentric circles toward the center of the room.

4 If you find a suspicious parcel or device, do not touch it—call the bomb squad.

Detection Devices

There are several types of devices and methods that can be used to identify bombs, including metal and vapor detectors, as well as X-ray machines. Several devices are portable and inexpensive enough for an individual to obtain.

Particulate Explosives Detector
- Detects modern plastic explosive constituents as well as TNT and nitroglycerin.
- Detects RDX (used in C4, PE4, SX2, Semtex, Demex, and Detasheet); PETN (used in certain military explosives and Semtex); TNT (trinitrotoluene), and NG (nitroglycerin).
- Uses IMS (ion mobility spectroscopy) to detect micron-size particles used in explosives. A sample size of one nanogram is sufficient for detection.
- To use, swipe the suspect material with a sample wipe or a cotton glove. Analysis time is approximately three seconds. A visual display contains a red warning light and an LCD, giving a graphic display with a relative numerical scale of the target materials identified. An audible alarm can be triggered based on a user-defined threshold.
- Requires AC or battery.
- Approximately 15 x 12 x 5 inches.

Portable X-Ray System
- Uses a Polaroid radiographic film cassette and processor to create detailed radiographs of parcels and packages.
- Requires AC or a rechargeable battery.
- To use, simply point the lens at the suspect item and use the processor to view the image on the film.

identifying a bomb

Spray Bomb Detector

This portable aerosol spray is used in conjunction with laminated test paper to detect explosives—both plastic and traditional TNT—on parcels and on hands and fingerprints. The test kit includes test paper and two spray cans, E and X.

First, rub the white paper over the desired surface (briefcase, suitcase, etc.) and then spray with the E canister. If TNT is detected, the paper turns violet. If no reaction occurs, spray the paper with the X canister. The immediate appearance of pink indicates plastic explosives.

Expray can also be sprayed directly on paper and parcels. The procedure and results are identical.

Bomb Range Detector

This detector of radio-controlled explosives is mounted in a car.

The unit automatically scans and transmits on every radio frequency in a one-kilometer radius. When a radio-controlled explosive is in the area, the device jams it to render it harmless.

Be Aware

All bomb experts stress that avoidance is the key concept when dealing with explosives. Your best chance of survival lies with the bomb squad, not with one of these devices.

HOW TO
DELIVER A BABY
IN A TAXICAB

Before you attempt to deliver a baby, use your best efforts to get to a hospital first. There really is no way to know exactly when the baby is ready to emerge, so even if you think you may not have time to get to the hospital, you probably do. Even the "water breaking" is not a sure sign that birth will happen immediately. The water is actually the amniotic fluid and the membrane that the baby floats in; birth can occur many hours after the mother's water breaks. However, if you leave too late or get stuck in crosstown traffic and you must deliver the baby on your own, here are the basic concepts.

1 **Time the uterine contractions.**
For first-time mothers, when contractions are about three to five minutes apart and last forty to ninety seconds—and increase in strength and frequency—for at least an hour, the labor is most likely real and not false (though it can be). Babies basically deliver themselves, and they will not come out of the womb until they are ready. Have clean, dry towels, a clean shirt, or something similar on hand.

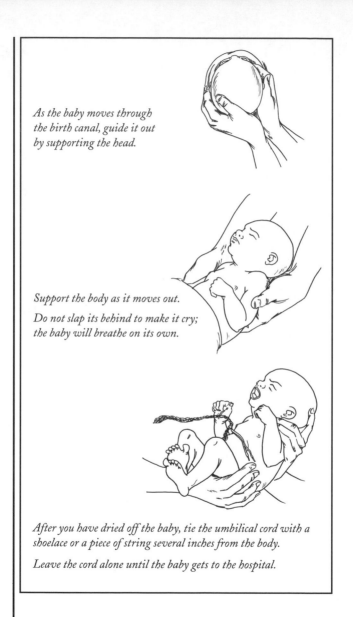

As the baby moves through the birth canal, guide it out by supporting the head.

Support the body as it moves out.

Do not slap its behind to make it cry; the baby will breathe on its own.

After you have dried off the baby, tie the umbilical cord with a shoelace or a piece of string several inches from the body.

Leave the cord alone until the baby gets to the hospital.

2 | As the baby moves out of the womb, its head—
the biggest part of its body—will open the cervix so
the rest of it can pass through.

(If feet are coming out first, see next page.) As the
baby moves through the birth canal and out of the
mother's body, guide it out by supporting the head
and then the body.

3 | When the baby is out of the mother, dry it off and
keep it warm.

Do not slap its behind to make it cry; the baby will
breathe on its own. If necessary, clear any fluid out of
the baby's mouth with your fingers.

4 | Tie off the umbilical cord.

Take a piece of string—a shoelace works well—and
tie off the cord several inches from the baby.

5 | It is not necessary to cut the umbilical cord, unless
you are hours away from the hospital.

In that event, you can safely cut the cord by tying it
in another place a few inches closer to the mother and
cutting it between the knots. Leave the cord alone
until you get to a hospital. The piece of the cord
attached to the baby will fall off by itself. The pla-
centa will follow the baby in as few as three or as
many as thirty minutes.

IF THE FEET COME FIRST

The most common complication during pregnancy is a breech baby, or one that is positioned so the feet, and not the head, will come out of the uterus first. Since the head is the largest part of the baby, the danger is that, if the feet come out first, the cervix may not be dilated enough to get the head out afterward. Today, most breech babies are delivered through cesarean sections, a surgical procedure that you will not be able to perform. If you have absolutely no alternatives (no hospital or doctors or midwives are available) when the baby begins to emerge, you can try to deliver the baby feet first. A breech birth does not necessarily mean that the head won't be able to get through the cervix; there is simply a higher possibility that this will occur. Deliver the baby as you would in the manner prescribed above.

HOW TO TREAT FROSTBITE

Frostbite is a condition caused by the freezing of water molecules in skin cells and occurs in very cold temperatures. It is characterized by white, waxy skin that feels numb and hard. More severe cases result in a bluish black skin color, and the most severe cases result in gangrene, which may lead to amputation. Affected areas are generally fingertips and toes, and the nose, ears, and cheeks. Frostbite should be treated by a doctor. However, in an emergency, take the following steps.

1 Remove wet clothing and dress the area with warm, dry clothing.

2 Immerse frozen areas in warm water (100–105° F) or apply warm compresses for ten to thirty minutes.

3 If warm water is not available, wrap gently in warm blankets.

4 Avoid direct heat, including electric or gas fires, heating pads, and hot water bottles.

5 Never thaw the area if it is at risk of refreezing; this can cause severe tissue damage.

treating frostbite

6 │ Do not rub frostbitten skin or rub snow on it.

7 │ Take a pain reliever such as aspirin or ibuprofen during rewarming to lessen the pain.
Rewarming will be accompanied by a severe burning sensation. There may be skin blistering and soft tissue swelling and the skin may turn red, blue, or purple in color. When skin is pink and no longer numb, the area is thawed.

8 │ Apply sterile dressings to the affected areas.
Place the dressing between fingers or toes if they have been affected. Try not to disturb any blisters, wrap rewarmed areas to prevent refreezing, and have the patient keep thawed areas as still as possible.

9 │ Get medical treatment as soon as possible.

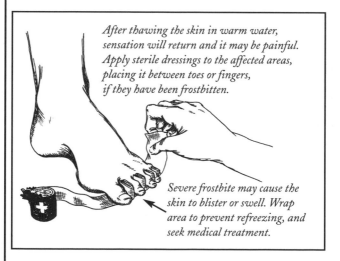

After thawing the skin in warm water, sensation will return and it may be painful. Apply sterile dressings to the affected areas, placing it between toes or fingers, if they have been frostbitten.

Severe frostbite may cause the skin to blister or swell. Wrap area to prevent refreezing, and seek medical treatment.

How to Treat Frostnip

Frostnip is the early warning sign of frostbite. Frostnip is characterized by numbness and a pale coloring of the affected areas. It can be safely treated at home.

1 Remove wet clothing.

2 Immerse or soak affected areas in warm water (100–105° F).

3 Do not allow patient to control water temperature—numb areas cannot feel heat and can be burned.

4 Continue treatment until skin is pink and sensation returns.

How to Avoid Frostbite and Frostnip

- Keep extremities warm and covered in cold weather.
- Use layered clothing and a face mask.
- Wear mittens instead of gloves, and keep the ears covered.
- Take regular breaks from the cold whenever possible to warm extremities.

HOW TO TREAT A LEG FRACTURE

Most leg injuries are only sprains, but the treatment for both sprains and fractures is the same.

1 | **If skin is broken, do not touch or put anything on the wound.**
You must avoid infection. If the wound is bleeding severely, try to stop the flow of blood by applying steady pressure to the affected area with sterile bandages or clean clothes.

2 | **Do not move the injured leg—you need to splint the wound to stabilize the injured area.**

3 | **Find two stiff objects of the same length—wood, plastic, or folded cardboard—for the splints.**

4 | **Put the splints above and below the injured area—under the leg (or on the side if moving the leg is too painful).**

5 | **Tie the splints with string, rope, or belts—whatever is available.**
Alternatively, use clothing torn into strips. Make sure the splint extends beyond the injured area.

6 | **Do not tie the splints too tightly; this may cut off circulation.**

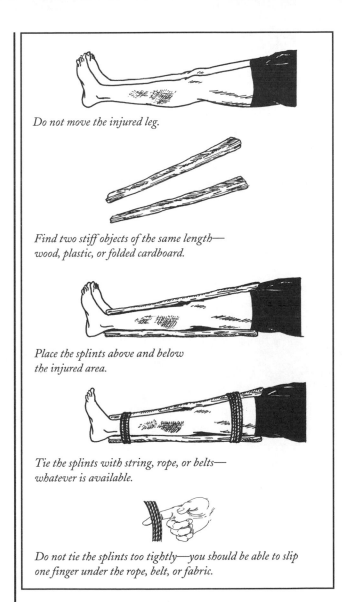

Do not move the injured leg.

Find two stiff objects of the same length—wood, plastic, or folded cardboard.

Place the splints above and below the injured area.

Tie the splints with string, rope, or belts—whatever is available.

Do not tie the splints too tightly—you should be able to slip one finger under the rope, belt, or fabric.

You should be able to slip a finger under the rope or fabric. If the splinted area becomes pale or white, loosen the ties.

7 | Have the injured person lie flat on their back. This helps blood continue to circulate and may prevent shock.

SYMPTOMS OF A FRACTURE, SPRAIN, OR DISLOCATION

- Difficult or limited movement
- Swelling
- Bruising of the affected area
- Severe pain
- Numbness
- Severe bleeding
- A visible break of bone through the skin

WHAT TO AVOID

- Do not push at, probe, or attempt to clean an injury; this can cause infection.
- Do not move the injured person unless absolutely necessary. Treat the fracture and then go get help.
- If the person must be moved, be sure the injury is completely immobilized first.
- Do not elevate a leg injury.
- Do not attempt to move or reset a broken bone; this will cause severe pain and may complicate the injury.

HOW TO TREAT
A BULLET OR
KNIFE WOUND

1 Do not immediately pull out any impaled objects.
Bullets, arrows, knives, sticks, and the like cause penetrating injuries. When these objects lodge in the vital
areas of the body (the trunk or near nerves or arteries) removing them may cause more severe bleeding
that cannot be controlled. The object may be pressed
against an artery or other vital internal structure and
may actually be helping to reduce the bleeding.

2 Control the bleeding by using a combination of
direct pressure, limb elevation, pressure points, and
tourniquets (in that order).
DIRECT PRESSURE. You can control most bleeding by
placing direct pressure on the wound. Attempt to
apply pressure directly to bleeding surfaces. The scalp,
for instance, bleeds profusely. Using your fingertips to
press the edges of a scalp wound against the underlying bone is more effective than using the palm of your
hand to apply pressure over a wider area. Use the tips
of your fingers to control bleeding arterioles (small
squirting vessels).

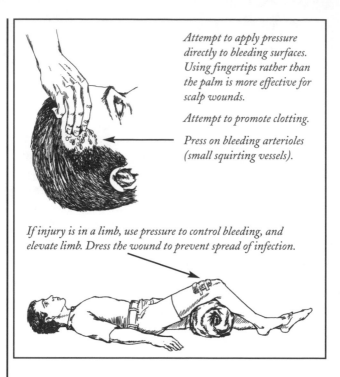

Attempt to apply pressure directly to bleeding surfaces. Using fingertips rather than the palm is more effective for scalp wounds.

Attempt to promote clotting.

Press on bleeding arterioles (small squirting vessels).

If injury is in a limb, use pressure to control bleeding, and elevate limb. Dress the wound to prevent spread of infection.

LIMB ELEVATION. When a wound is in an extremity, elevation of the extremity above the heart, in addition to direct pressure, may reduce the bleeding further. Never make people who are in shock sit up simply to elevate a bleeding wound.

PRESSURE POINTS. To reduce blood flow you usually have to compress an artery (where you can feel the pulse) near the wound against an underlying bone. Just pressing into the soft belly of a muscle does not reduce blood flow by this mechanism.

Tourniquets. A tourniquet is a wide band of cloth or a belt that is placed around an extremity and tightened (usually using a windlass) until the blood flow is cut off. The blood supply must be compressed against a long bone (the upper arm or upper leg) since vessels between the double bones in the lower arm and lower leg will continue to bleed despite a tourniquet. The amount of pressure necessary typically causes additional vascular and nerve trauma that is permanent. A tourniquet should only be used as a last resort—to save a life at the expense of sacrificing a limb.

3 | Immobilize the injured area.
Using splints and dressings to immobilize an injured area helps protect from further injury and maintain clots that have begun to form. Even if an injury to a bone or joint is not suspected, immobilization will promote clotting and help healing begin.

4 | Dress the wound, and strive to prevent infection.
Use sterile (or at least clean) dressings as much as possible. Penetrating injuries may allow anaerobic (air-hating) bacteria to get deep into the tissue. This is why penetrating wounds are typically irrigated with sterile or antibiotic solutions in surgery. While this is rarely practical outside of the hospital, it is important to remember that smaller penetrating wounds (nail holes in the foot and the like) should be encouraged to bleed for a short period to help "wash out" foreign material. Soaking an extremity in hydrogen peroxide may help kill anaerobic bacteria as well. Do not apply

ointments or goo to penetrating wounds as these may actually promote infection.

Emergency Tip

Some data indicate that pure granular sugar poured into a penetrating wound can decrease bleeding, promote clotting, and discourage bacteria. You are not likely to see it used in your local emergency department, but it might be worth consideration if your circumstances are dire.

5 Get medical attention as soon as possible.

Be Aware

It should be noted that tourniquets are rarely helpful—it is uncommon to have life-threatening bleeding in an extremity that cannot be controlled by the methods described above. The areas that cause fatal bleeding (like the femoral arteries or intra-abdominal bleeding) do not lend themselves to the use of a tourniquet. Even most complete amputations do not bleed all that much, and are controlled by direct pressure. Arteries that are severed only part of the way through tend to bleed more profusely than those that are completely severed.

CHAPTER 5
ADVENTURE SURVIVAL

HOW TO LAND A PLANE

These instructions cover small passenger planes and jets (not commercial airliners).

1   If the plane has only one set of controls, push, pull, carry, or drag the pilot out of the pilot's seat.

2   Take your place at the controls.

3   Put on the radio headset (if there is one).
Use the radio to call for help—there will be a control button on the yoke (the plane's steering wheel) or a CB-like microphone on the instrument panel. Depress the button to talk, release it to listen. Say "Mayday! Mayday!" and give your situation, destination, and plane call numbers, which should be printed on the top of the instrument panel.

4   If you get no response, try again on the emergency channel—tune the radio to 121.5.
All radios are different, but tuning is standard. The person on the other end should be able to talk you through the proper landing procedures. Follow their instructions carefully. If you cannot reach someone to talk you through the landing process, you will have to do it alone.

5   **Get your bearings and identify the instruments.**
Look around you. Is the plane level? Unless you have just taken off or are about to land, it should be flying relatively straight.

YOKE. This is the steering wheel and should be in front of you. It turns the plane and controls its pitch. Pull back on the column to bring the nose up, push forward to point it down. Turn left to turn the plane left, turn right to turn it right. The yoke is very sensitive—move it only an inch or two in either direction to turn the plane in flight. While cruising, the nose of the plane should be about three inches below the horizon.

ALTIMETER. This is the most important instrument, at least initially. It is a red dial in the middle of the instrument panel that indicates altitude: the small hand indicates feet above sea level in thousand-foot increments, the large hand in hundreds.

HEADING. This is a compass and will be the only instrument with a small image of a plane in the center. The nose will point in the direction the plane is headed.

AIRSPEED. This dial is on the top of the instrument panel and will be on the left. It is usually calibrated in knots, though it may also have miles per hour. A small plane travels at about 120 knots while cruising. Anything under 70 knots in the air is dangerously close to stall speed. (A knot is $1\frac{1}{4}$ miles per hour.)

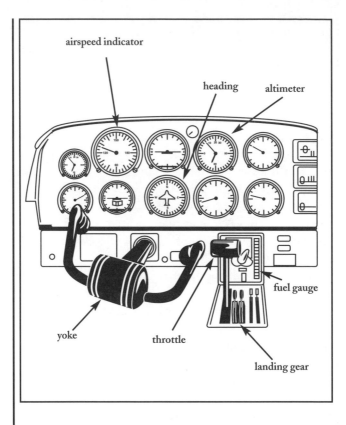

airspeed indicator

heading altimeter

yoke

throttle

fuel gauge

landing gear

THROTTLE. This controls airspeed (power) and also the nose attitude, or its relation to the horizon. It is a lever between the seats and is always black. Pull it toward you to slow the plane and cause it to descend, push it away to speed up the plane and cause it to ascend. The engine will get more or less quiet depending on the direction the throttle is moved.

Fuel. The fuel gauges will be on the lower portion of the instrument panel. If the pilot has followed FAA regulations, the plane should have enough fuel for the amount of flying time to your intended destination plus at least an additional half hour in reserve. Some planes have a reserve fuel tank in addition to the primary one, but do not worry about changing tanks.

Flaps. Due to their complexity, wing flaps can make the plane harder to control. Use the throttle to control airspeed, not the flaps.

6 Begin the descent.
Pull back on the throttle to slow down. Reduce power by about one-quarter of cruising speed. As the plane slows, the nose will drop. For descent, the nose should be about four inches below the horizon.

7 Deploy the landing gear.
Determine if the plane has fixed or retractable landing gear. Fixed landing gear is always down so you need do nothing. If it is retractable, there will be another lever between the seats near the throttle, with a handle that is shaped like a tire. For a water landing, leave the landing gear up (retracted).

8 Look for a suitable landing site.
If you cannot find an airport, find a flat field on which to land. A mile-long field is ideal, but finding a field of this length will be difficult unless you are in the Midwest. The plane can land on a much shorter

strip of earth, so do not bother to look for the "perfect" landing site—there is no such thing. Bumpy terrain will also do if your options are limited.

9   **Line up the landing strip so that when the altimeter reads one thousand feet the field is off the right-wing tip.**
In an ideal situation, you should take a single pass over the field to look for obstructions; with plenty of fuel, you may want to do so. Fly over the field, make a big rectangle, and approach a second time.

10   **When approaching the landing strip, reduce power by pulling back on the throttle.**
Do not let the nose drop more than six inches below the horizon.

11   **The plane should be one hundred feet off the ground when you are just above the landing strip, and the rear wheels should touch first.**
The plane will stall at fifty-five to sixty-five miles per hour, and you want the plane to be at just about stall speed when the wheels touch the ground.

12   **Pull all the way back on the throttle, and make sure the nose of the plane does not dip too steeply.**
Gently pull back on the yoke as the plane slowly touches the ground.

13   **Using the pedals on the floor, steer and brake the plane as needed.**

The yoke has very little effect on the ground. The upper pedals are the brakes, and the lower pedals control the direction of the nose wheel. Concentrate first on the lower pedals. Press the right pedal to move the plane right, press the left pedal to move it left. Upon landing, be aware of your speed. A modest reduction in speed will increase your chances of survival exponentially. By reducing your groundspeed from 120 to 70 miles per hour, you increase your chance of survival threefold.

Be Aware

- A well-executed emergency landing in bad terrain can be less hazardous than an uncontrolled landing on an established field.
- If the plane is headed toward trees, steer it between them so the wings absorb the impact if you hit.
- When the plane comes to a stop, get out as soon as possible and get away—and take the pilot with you.

HOW TO SURVIVE
AN EARTHQUAKE

1 If you are indoors, stay there!
Get under a desk or table and hang on to it, or move into a doorway; the next best place is in a hallway or against an inside wall. Stay clear of windows, fire-places, and heavy furniture or appliances. Get out of the kitchen, which is a dangerous place. Do not run downstairs or rush outside while the building is shaking or while there is danger of falling and hurting yourself or being hit by falling glass or debris.

2 If you are outside, get into the open, away from buildings, power lines, chimneys, and anything else that might fall on you.

3 If you are driving, stop, but carefully.
Move your car as far out of traffic as possible. Do not stop on or under a bridge or overpass or under trees, light posts, power lines, or signs. Stay inside your car until the shaking stops. When you resume driving watch for breaks in the pavement, fallen rocks, and bumps in the road at bridge approaches.

4 If you are in a mountainous area, watch out for falling rocks, landslides, trees, and other debris that could be loosened by quakes.

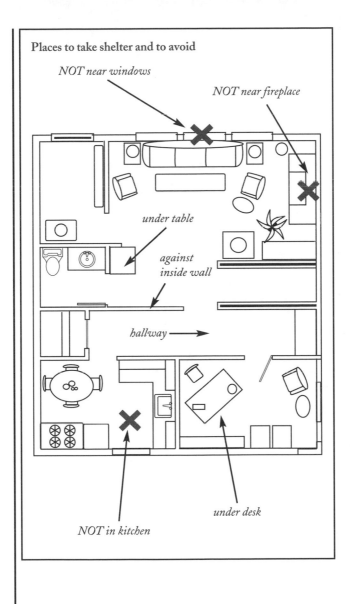

Places to take shelter and to avoid

NOT near windows

NOT near fireplace

under table

against inside wall

hallway →

NOT in kitchen

under desk

5 After the quake stops, check for injuries and apply the necessary first aid or seek help.
Do not attempt to move seriously injured persons unless they are in further danger of injury. Cover them with blankets and seek medical help for serious injuries.

6 If you can, put on a pair of sturdy thick-soled shoes (in case you step on broken glass, debris, etc.).

7 Check for hazards.
- Put out fires in your home or neighborhood immediately.
- Gas leaks: shut off main gas valve only if you suspect a leak because of broken pipes or odor. Do not use matches, lighters, camp stoves or barbecues, electrical equipment, or appliances until you are sure there are no gas leaks. They may create a spark that could ignite leaking gas and cause an explosion and fire. Do not turn on the gas again if you turned it off—let the gas company do it.
- Damaged electrical wiring: shut off power at the control box if there is any danger to house wiring.
- Downed or damaged utility lines: do not touch downed power lines or any objects in contact with them.
- Spills: clean up any spilled medicines, drugs, or other harmful materials such as bleach, lye, or gas.

- Downed or damaged chimneys: approach with caution and do not use a damaged chimney (it could start a fire or let poisonous gases into your house).
- Fallen items: beware of items tumbling off shelves when you open closet and cupboard doors.

8 **Check food and water supplies.**
Do not eat or drink anything from open containers near shattered glass. If the power is off, plan meals to use up frozen foods or foods that will spoil quickly. Food in the freezer should be good for at least a couple of days. If the water is off you can drink from water heaters, melted ice cubes, or canned vegetables. Avoid drinking water from swimming pools and spas.

9 **Be prepared for aftershocks.**
Another quake, larger or smaller, may follow.

Be Aware
- Use your telephone only for a medical or fire emergency—you could tie up the lines needed for emergency response. If the phone doesn't work, send someone for help.
- Do not expect firefighters, police, or paramedics to help you immediately. They may not be available.

How to Prepare

Being prepared for an earthquake is the best way to survive one. Make sure each member of the household knows what to do no matter where they are when a quake occurs:

- Establish a meeting place where you can reunite afterward.
- Find out about earthquake plans developed by your children's school or day care.
- Transportation may be disrupted, so keep emergency supplies—food, liquids, and comfortable shoes, for example—at work.
- Know where your gas, electric, and water main shutoffs are and how to turn them off if there is a leak or electrical short. Make sure older members of the family can shut off utilities.
- Locate your nearest fire and police stations and emergency medical facility.
- Talk to your neighbors—you can help one another during and after an earthquake.
- Take Red Cross first aid and CPR training courses.

HOW TO SURVIVE ADRIFT AT SEA

1 Stay aboard your boat as long as possible before you get into a life raft.

In a maritime emergency, the rule of thumb is that you should step up into your raft, meaning you should be up to your waist in water before you get into the raft. Your best chance of survival is on a boat—even a disabled one—not on a life raft. But if the boat is sinking, know how to use a life raft. Any craft that sails in open water (a boat larger than fourteen feet) should have at least one life raft. Smaller boats may only have life jackets, so these vessels should stay within easy swimming distance of land.

2 Get in the life raft, and take whatever supplies you can carry.

Most importantly, if you have water in jugs, take it with you. Do not drink seawater. A person can last for several days without food at sea, but without clean water to drink, death is a virtual certainty within several days. If worse comes to worst, throw the jugs of water overboard so that you can get them later—they will float.

Many canned foods, particularly vegetables, are packed in water, so take those with you if you can. Do not ration water; drink it as needed, but don't drink more than is necessary—a half-gallon a day should be sufficient if you limit your activity.

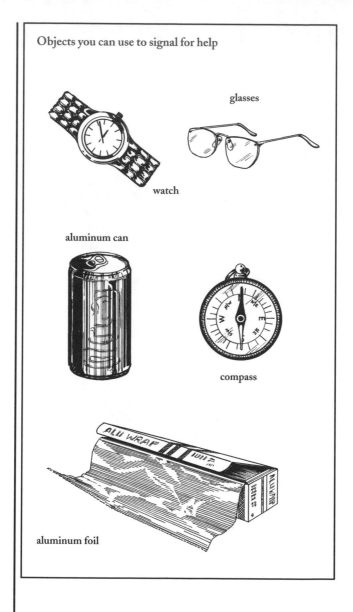

Objects you can use to signal for help

glasses

watch

aluminum can

compass

ALU WRAP

aluminum foil

3 If you are in a cold water/weather environment, get warm.
You are more likely to die of exposure or hypothermia than of anything else.

Put on dry clothes and stay out of the water. Prolonged exposure to saltwater can damage your skin and cause lesions, which are prone to infection.

Stay covered. Modern life rafts have canopies, which protect passengers from sun, wind, and rain. If the canopy is missing or damaged, wear a hat, long sleeves, and pants to protect yourself from the sun.

4 Find food, if you can.
Life rafts include fishing hooks in their survival kits. If your raft is floating for several weeks, seaweed will form on its underside and fish will naturally congregate in the shade under you. You can catch them with the hook and eat the flesh raw. If no hook is available, you can fashion one using wire or even shards of aluminum from an empty can.

5 Try to get to land, if you know where it is.
Most rafts include small paddles, but life rafts are not very maneuverable, especially in any wind above three knots. Do not exhaust yourself—you will not be able to move any significant distance without great effort.

6 If you see a plane or boat nearby, try to signal them.
Use a VHF radio or a handheld flare kit to get their attention. A small mirror can also be used for signaling.

How to Prepare

Never go out on a boat unprepared. Most boats should have at least one type of emergency signaling device, which is called an Emergency Position Radio Beacon, or EPiRB. These devices send out global marine distress signals and come in two forms: 406 MHz and 125 MHz. Both will send your boat identification and position, but the 406 goes to other ships, passing airplanes, and satellites, while the 125 only goes to ships and planes. People without one of these devices can drift for months before they are found.

Always carry a "go bag" that contains:
• Warm, dry clothes and blankets
• A hat
• Food (canned goods, backpacking foods, dried fruit)
• A handheld VHF radio
• A small, handheld GPS (Global Positioning Satellite) tracking unit
• Drinking water in portable jugs
• A compass
• A flashlight with extra batteries
• Handheld flares
• A handheld watermaker

HOW TO SURVIVE WHEN LOST IN THE DESERT

1 Do not panic, especially if people know where you are and when you are scheduled to return.
If you have a vehicle, stay with it—do not wander!

2 If you are on foot, try to backtrack by retracing your steps.
Always move downstream or down country. Travel along ridges instead of in washes or valleys, where it is harder for you to see and for rescuers to see you.

3 If you have completely lost your bearings, try to get to a high vista and look around.
If you are not absolutely sure you can follow your tracks or prints, stay put.

4 Build smoky fires during daylight hours (tires work well) but keep a bright fire burning at night.
If fuel is limited, keep a small kindling-fire burning and have fuel ready to burn if you spot a person or vehicle.

5 If a car or plane is passing, or if you see other people off in the distance, try to signal them with one of the following methods:

In a clearing, you can use newspaper or aluminum foil weighed down with rocks to make a large triangle; this is the international distress symbol.

- A large I indicates to rescuers that someone is injured.
- An X means you are unable to proceed.
- An F indicates you need food and water.
- Three shots from a gun is another recognized distress signal.

6 To avoid heat prostration, rest frequently.

Deserts in the United States can reach temperatures upwards of 120 degrees during the day, and shade can be scarce. In the summer, sit at least twelve inches above the ground on a stool or a branch (ground temperatures can be thirty degrees hotter than the surrounding air temperature).

When walking during daylight hours:

- Walk slowly to conserve energy and rest at least ten minutes every hour.
- Drink water; don't ration it.
- Avoid talking and smoking.
- Breathe through your nose, not your mouth.
- Avoid alcohol, which dehydrates.
- Avoid eating if there is not a sufficient amount of water readily available; digestion consumes water.
- Stay in the shade and wear clothing, including a shirt, hat, and sunglasses. Clothing helps ration sweat by slowing evaporation and prolonging cooling.

- Travel in the evening, at night, or early in the day.
- In cold weather, wear layers of clothing, and make sure you and your clothes are dry.
- Watch for signs of hypothermia, which include intense shivering, muscle tensing, fatigue, poor coordination, stumbling, and blueness of the lips and fingernails. If you see these signs, get dry clothing on immediately and light a fire if possible. If not, huddle close to companions for warmth.

7 Try to find water. The best places to look are:
- The base of rock cliffs.
- In the gravel wash from mountain valleys, especially after a recent rain.
- The outside edge of a sharp bend in a dry streambed. Look for wet sand, then dig down three to six feet to find seeping water.
- Near green vegetation. Tree clusters and other shrubbery, such as cottonwood, sycamore, or willow trees, may indicate the presence of water.
- Animal paths and flocks of birds. Following them may lead you to water.

8 Find cactus fruit and flowers.
Split open the base of cactus stalks and chew on the pith, but don't swallow it. Carry chunks of pith to alleviate thirst while walking. Other desert plants are inedible and will make you sick.

Where to Find Water

Base of rock cliffs

The outside edge of dry streambeds

Gravel wash from mountain valleys

Green vegetation such as sycamore trees or other shrubbery

Cactus fruit or flowers can be eaten. Split open the base and chew on the pith.

surviving when lost in the desert

How to Prepare

When planning a trip to a desert area that is sparsely populated, always inform someone of your destination, the duration of the trip, and its intended route. Leaving without alerting anyone and getting lost means no one will be looking for you.

If traveling by car, make sure your vehicle is in good condition, and make sure you have:

- A sound battery
- Good hoses (squeeze them: they should be firm, not soft and mushy)
- A spare tire with the proper inflation
- Spare fan belts
- Tools
- Reserve gasoline and oil
- Water (five gallons for a vehicle)

How to Drive Safely

Keep an eye on the sky. Flash floods can occur in a wash any time thunderheads are in sight, even though it may not be raining where you are. If you get caught in a dust storm while driving, get off the road immediately. Turn off your driving lights and turn on your emergency flashers. Back into the wind to reduce windshield pitting by sand particles. Before driving through washes and sandy areas, test the footing. One minute on foot may save hours of hard work and prevent a punctured oil pan.

If your vehicle breaks down, stay near it; your emergency supplies are there. Raise the hood and trunk lid to denote "help needed." A vehicle can be seen for miles, but a person is very difficult to find.

- Leave a disabled vehicle only if you are positive of the route to help.
- If stalled or lost, set signal fires. Set smoky fires in the daytime, bright ones for the night. Three fires in a triangle denotes "help needed."
- If you find a road, stay on it.

WHAT TO BRING
WHEN TRAVELING BY FOOT

- Water (one gallon per person per day is adequate; two or more gallons is smarter and safer)
- A map that shows the nearest populated areas
- Waterproof matches
- A cigarette lighter or flint and steel
- A survival guide
- Strong sunscreen, a hat, warm clothes, and blankets
- A pocket knife
- A metal signaling mirror
- Iodine tablets
- A small pencil and writing materials
- A whistle (three blasts denotes "help needed")
- A canteen cup
- Aluminum foil
- A compass
- A first aid kit

surviving when lost in the desert

How to Avoid Getting Lost

- When hiking, periodically look back in the direction from where you have come. Taking a mental picture of what it will look like when you return helps in case you become lost.
- Stay on established trails if possible and mark the trail route with blazes on trees and brush, or by making *ducques* (pronounced "ducks"), which are piles of three rocks stacked on top of one another.

HOW TO SURVIVE IF YOUR PARACHUTE FAILS TO OPEN

1 As soon as you realize that your chute is bad, signal to a jumping companion whose chute has not yet opened that you are having a malfunction.
Wave your arms and point to your chute.

2 When your companion (and new best friend) gets to you, hook arms.

3 Once you are hooked together, the two of you will still be falling at terminal velocity, or about 130 miles per hour.
When your friend opens his chute, there will be no way either of you will be able hold on to one another normally, because the G-forces will triple or quadruple your body weight. To prepare for this problem, hook your arms into his chest strap, or through the two sides of the front of his harness, all the way up to your elbows, and grab hold of your own strap.

4 Open the chute.
The chute opening shock will be severe, probably enough to dislocate or break your arms.

Hook arms with your companion. Then hook your arms into his chest strap, up to the elbows, and grab hold of your own.

5 Steer the canopy.

Your friend must now hold on to you with one arm while steering his canopy (the part of the chute that controls direction and speed).

If your friend's canopy is slow and big, you may hit the grass or dirt slowly enough to break only a leg, and your chances of survival are high.

If his canopy is a fast one, however, your friend will have to steer to avoid hitting the ground too fast. You must also avoid power lines and other obstructions at all costs.

6 | **If there is a body of water nearby, head for that.**
Of course, once you hit the water, you will have to tread with just your legs and hope that your partner is able to pull you out before your chute takes in water.

How to Prepare

Check your chute before you jump. The good news is that today's parachutes are built to open, so even if you make big mistakes packing them, they tend to sort themselves out. The reserve chute, however, must be packed by a certified rigger and must be perfect as it is your last resort. Make sure that:

- The parachute is folded in straight lines—that there are no twists.
- The slider is positioned correctly to keep the parachute from opening too fast.

HOW TO SURVIVE
AN AVALANCHE

1 Struggle to stay on top of the snow by using a freestyle swimming motion.

2 If you are buried, your best chance of survival is if someone saw you get covered.

The snow in an avalanche is like a wet snowball: it is not light and powdery, and once you are buried, it is very difficult to dig your way out.

3 If you are only partially buried, you can dig your way out with your hands or by kicking at the snow. If you still have a ski pole, poke through the snow in several directions until you see or feel open air, then dig in that direction.

4 If you are completely buried, chances are you will be too injured to help yourself.

However, if you are able, dig a small hole around you and spit in it. The saliva should head downhill, giving you an idea of which direction is up. Dig up, and do it quickly.

Be Aware
- Never go hiking or skiing alone in avalanche territory.
- Carry an avalanche probe—a sturdy, sectional aluminum pole that fits together to create a probe

Struggle to stay on top of the snow by using a freestyle swimming motion.

six to eight feet in length. Some ski poles are threaded and can be screwed together to form avalanche probes.

- Know where and when avalanches are likely to occur.
- Avalanches occur in areas with new snow; on the non-leeward side of mountains (the leeward side is the side facing the wind); and in the afternoons of sunny days, when the morning sun may have

loosened the snowpack. They occur most often on mountainsides with angles of thirty to forty-five degrees—these are often the most popular slopes for skiing.

- Avalanches can be triggered by numerous factors, including recent snowfall, wind, and sunlight. As new snow accumulates with successive storms, the layers may be of different consistencies and not bond to one another, making the snow highly unstable.
- Loud noises do not cause avalanches except if they cause significant vibrations in the ground or snow.
- The activity with the highest avalanche risk is now snowmobiling. Snowmobiles—sometimes called mountain sleds—are powerful and light, and can get high into mountainous terrain, where avalanches occur.
- Carry a beacon. The beacon broadcasts your position by setting up a magnetic field that can be picked up by the other beacons in your group. If skiing on a dangerous slope, go down one at a time, not as a group, in case a slide occurs.

How to Rescue Others

If you have witnessed others being buried by an avalanche, contact the ski patrol as soon as possible. Then search first by trees and benches—the places where people are most commonly buried. All searchers should have small, collapsible shovels to help them dig quickly if they find someone.

HOW TO SURVIVE IF YOU ARE IN THE LINE OF GUNFIRE

IF YOU ARE THE PRIMARY TARGET

1 Get as far away as possible.
An untrained shooter isn't likely to be accurate at any distance greater than sixty feet.

2 Run fast, but do not move in a straight line—weave back and forth to make it more difficult for the shooter to draw a bead on you.
The average shooter will not have the training necessary to hit a moving target at any real distance.

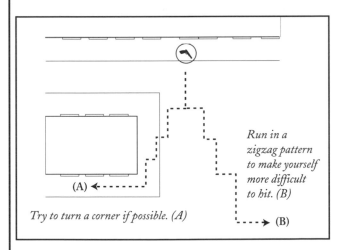

Run in a zigzag pattern to make yourself more difficult to hit. (B)

(A) ◄- - - - -

Try to turn a corner if possible. (A)

- - - ► (B)

3 | Do not bother to count shots.
You will have no idea if the shooter has more ammunition. Counting is only for the movies.

4 | Turn a corner as quickly as you can, particularly if your pursuer has a rifle or assault weapon.
Rifles have much greater accuracy and range, and the person may be more likely to either aim or spray bullets in your direction.

If You Are Not the Primary Target

1 | Get down, and stay down.
If the intended target is near you or if the shooter is firing at random, get as low as possible. Do not crouch down; get flat on your stomach and stay there.

2 | If you are outside and can get to a car, run to it and lie behind a tire on the opposite side of the car from the shooter.
If no cars are present, lie in the gutter next to the curb. A car will stop or deflect a small-caliber bullet fired toward you. However, higher caliber bullets—such as those from an assault rifle or bullets that are designed to pierce armor—can easily penetrate a car and hit someone on the opposite side.

3 | If you are inside a building and the shooter is inside, get to another room and lie flat.

If you cannot get to another room, move behind any heavy, thick objects (a solid desk, filing cabinets, tables, a couch) for protection.

4 If you are face-to-face with the shooter, do anything you can to make yourself less of a target.
Turn sideways, and stay low—stray bullets are likely to be at least a few feet above the ground. If the shooter is outside, stay inside and stay away from doors and windows.

5 Stay down until the shooting stops or until authorities arrive and give the all clear.

Attempt to keep large objects between you and the shooter.

HOW TO SURVIVE WHEN LOST IN THE MOUNTAINS

The number one cause of death when lost in the mountains is hypothermia—humans are basically tropical animals. Staying calm in the face of darkness, loneliness, and the unknown will greatly increase your chances of survival. Eighty percent of mountain survival is your reaction to fear, 10 percent is your survival gear, and the other 10 percent is knowing how to use it. Always tell someone else where you are going and when you will return.

1 **Do not panic.**
If you told someone where you were going, search and rescue teams will be looking for you. (In general, teams will search only during daylight hours for adults, but will search around the clock for children who are alone.)

2 **Find shelter, and stay warm and dry.**
Exerting yourself unnecessarily—like dragging heavy logs to build a shelter—will make you sweat and make you cold. Use the shelter around you before trying to construct one. If you are in a snow-covered area, you may be able to dig a cave in deep snow for shelter and protection from the wind. A snow trench may be a better idea—it requires less exertion. Simply use

In snow-covered country, build a snow cave or a snow trench for shelter and warmth. Use dead leaves and branches for insulation.

something to dig a trench, get in it, and cover it with branches or leaves. You should attempt to make your shelter in the middle of the mountain if possible. Stay out of the valleys—cold air falls, and the valley floor can be the coldest spot on the mountain.

3

Signal rescuers for help.
The best time to signal rescuers is during the day, with a signaling device or three fires in a triangle. Signal for help from the highest point possible—it will be easier for rescuers to see you, and any sound you make will travel farther. Build three smoky fires and put your blanket—gold side facing out, if it is a space blanket—on the ground.

4 | **Do not wander far.**
It will make finding you more difficult, as search teams will be trying to retrace your path and may miss you if you have gone off in a different direction. Searchers often wind up finding a vehicle with no one in it because the driver has wandered off.

5 | **If you get frostbite, do not rewarm the affected area until you're out of danger.**
You can walk on frostbitten feet, but once you warm the area and can feel the pain, you will not want to walk anywhere. Try to protect the frostbitten area and keep it dry until you are rescued.

How to Prepare

You must dress properly before entering a wilderness area. Layer your clothing in the following manner:

First (inner) layer: long underwear, preferably polypropylene. This provides only slight insulation—its purpose is to draw moisture off your skin.

Second (middle) layer: something to trap and create warm "dead air" space, such as a down parka.

Third (outer) layer: a Gore-Tex or other brand of breathable jacket that allows moisture out but not in. Dry insulation is key to your survival. Once you are wet, it is very difficult to get dry.

Make sure you have the following items in your survival kit, and that you know how to use them (reading the instructions for the first time in the dark wilderness is not recommended):

A HEAT SOURCE. Bring several boxes of waterproof matches, as well as a lighter. Trioxane—a small, light, chemical heat source that the Army uses—is recommended. Trioxane packs can be picked up in outdoor and military surplus stores. Dryer lint is also highly flammable and very lightweight.

SHELTER. Carry a small space blanket, which has a foil-like coating that insulates you. Get one that is silver on one side (for warmth) and orange-gold on the other, which can be used for signaling. The silver side is not a good color to signal with. It can be mistaken for ice or mineral rock. The orange-gold color does not occur in nature and will not be mistaken for anything else.

A SIGNALING DEVICE. A small mirror works well, as do flares or a whistle, which carries much farther than a voice.

FOOD. Pack carbohydrates: bagels, trail mix, granola bars, and so on. Proteins need heat to break down and require more water for digestion.

HOW TO MAKE FIRE WITHOUT MATCHES

WHAT YOU WILL NEED

- Knife
- Kindling. Several pieces, varying in size from small to large.
- Wood to keep the fire going. Select deadwood from the tree, not off the ground. Good wood should indent with pressure from a fingernail, but not break easily.
- Bow. A curved stick about two feet long.
- String. A shoelace, parachute cord, or leather thong. Primitive cordage can be made from yucca, milkweed, or another tough, stringy plant.
- Socket. A horn, bone, piece of hard wood, rock, or seashell that fits in the palm of the hand and will be placed over a stick.
- Lube. You can use earwax, skin oil, a ball of green grass, lip balm, or anything else oily.
- Spindle. A dry, straight $3/4$- to 1-inch-diameter stick approximately 12 to 18 inches long. Round one end and carve the other end to a point.
- Fire board. Select and shape a second piece of wood into a board approximately $3/4$ to 1 inch thick, 2 to 3 inches wide, and 10 to 12 inches long. Carve a shallow dish in the center of the flat side approximately

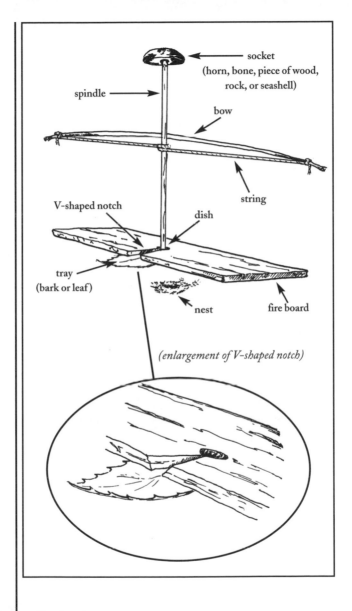

socket
(horn, bone, piece of wood,
rock, or seashell)

spindle

bow

string

V-shaped notch

dish

tray
(bark or leaf)

nest

fire board

(enlargement of V-shaped notch)

$^1/_2$ inch from the edge. Into the edge of this dish, cut a V-shaped notch.

- Tray. A piece of bark or leaf inserted under the V-shaped notch to catch the ember. The tray should not be made of deadwood.
- Nest. Dry bark, grass, leaves, cattail fuzz, or some other combustible material, formed into a bird nest shape.

How to Start the Fire

1 Tie the string tightly to the bow, one end to each end of the stick.

2 Kneel on your right knee, with the ball of your left foot on the fire board, holding it firmly to the ground.

3 Take the bow in your hands.

4 Loop the string in the center of the bow.

5 Insert the spindle in the loop of the bowstring so that the spindle is on the outside of the bow, pointed end up.
The bowstring should now be tight—if not, loop the string around the spindle a few more times.

6 Take the hand socket in your left hand, notch side down. Lubricate the notch.

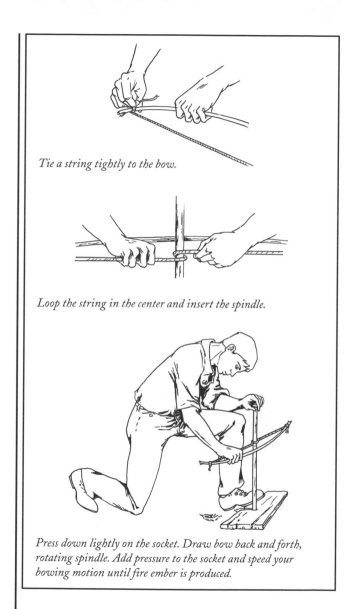

Tie a string tightly to the bow.

Loop the string in the center and insert the spindle.

Press down lightly on the socket. Draw bow back and forth, rotating spindle. Add pressure to the socket and speed your bowing motion until fire ember is produced.

7 Place the rounded end of the spindle into the dish of the fire board and the pointed end of the spindle into the hand socket.

8 Pressing down lightly on the socket, draw the bow back and forth, rotating the spindle slowly.

9 Add pressure to the socket and speed to your bowing until you begin to produce smoke and ash.
When there is a lot of smoke, you have created a fire ember.

10 Immediately stop your bowing motion and tap the spindle on the fire board to knock the ember into the tray.

11 Remove the tray and transfer the ember into your "nest."

12 Hold the nest tightly and blow steadily onto the ember. Eventually, the nest will catch fire.

13 Add kindling onto the nest. When the kindling catches, gradually add larger pieces of fuel.

Be Aware

You should not be dependent on any primitive fire method to maintain life in a wilderness survival emergency. Making fire in this manner can be quite difficult under actual harsh conditions (rain, snow, cold).

You should practice this method at home before you attempt it in the wilderness to familiarize yourself with the quirks of the process.

HOW TO AVOID BEING STRUCK BY LIGHTNING

Lightning causes more casualties annually in the U.S. than any other storm-related phenomenon except floods. No place is completely safe from lightning. However, some places are more dangerous than others.

1 **Loud or frequent thunder indicates that lightning activity is approaching.**
If you can see lightning and/or hear thunder, you are at risk. High winds, rainfall, and cloud cover often act as precursors to actual cloud-to-ground strikes. Thunderstorms generally move west to east and occur late in the day or in early evening when humidity is highest.

2 **When you see lightning, count the number of seconds until thunder is heard and then divide by five.** This will indicate how far the storm is from you in miles. (Sound travels at 1,100 feet per second.)

3 **If the time delay between seeing the flash (lightning) and hearing the boom (thunder) is fewer than thirty seconds, seek a safer location immediately.**
- Avoid high places, open fields, and ridges above the timberline. If in an open area, do not lie flat—kneel with your hands on the ground and your head low. If you are on a technical climb, sit on a rock

If you are in an open area, do not lie flat. Kneel with your hands on the ground and your head low.

DO NOT stand under a tree.

or on nonmetallic equipment. Tie a rope around your ankle; this will anchor you if a strike occurs and you are knocked off balance.

- Avoid isolated trees, unprotected gazebos, and rain or picnic shelters, as well as shallow depressions in the earth—current traveling through the ground may use you to bridge the depression.
- Avoid baseball dugouts, communications towers, flagpoles, light poles, metal and wood bleachers, and metal fences. If you are camping, avoid your tent if it is in an open area or under a large tree.
- Avoid golf carts and convertibles.
- Avoid bodies of water: oceans, lakes, swimming pools, and rivers.

4 Wait for the storm to pass.
The lightning threat generally diminishes with time after the last sound of thunder, but may persist for more than 30 minutes. When thunderstorms are in the area but not overhead, the lightning threat can exist even when it is sunny, not raining, or when clear sky is visible.

Be Aware
- Large enclosed buildings tend to be much safer than smaller or open structures. The risk for lightning injury depends on whether the structure incorporates lightning protection, the construction materials used, and the size of the structure.
- Fully enclosed metal vehicles such as cars, trucks, buses, vans, and fully enclosed farm vehicles with

the windows rolled up provide good shelter from lightning. Avoid contact with metal or conducting surfaces outside or inside the vehicle.

- When inside, avoid contact with conductive surfaces with exposure to the outside, including the shower, sink, plumbing fixtures, and metal door and window frames.
- Avoid outlets, electrical cords, and wired electrical devices, including telephones, computers, and televisions (particularly cable TVs).

How to Treat Someone Struck by Lightning

1 **Call 911 to report the strike and give directions to emergency personnel.**

With immediate medical treatment, victims can survive an encounter with lightning. If multiple people have been struck, treat the apparently "dead" first. People who are unconscious but still breathing will probably recover on their own.

2 **Move to a safer location to avoid getting struck yourself.**

It is unusual for victims who survive a lightning strike to have major fractures that would cause paralysis or major bleeding complications unless they have suffered a fall or been thrown a distance. Do not be afraid to move the victim rapidly if necessary; individuals struck by lightning do not carry a charge and it is safe to touch them to give medical treatment.

3 In cold and wet environments, put a protective layer between the victim and the ground to decrease the chance of hypothermia, which can further complicate resuscitation.
Check for burns, especially around jewelry and watches.

4 If the victim is not breathing, start mouth-to-mouth resuscitation.
Give one breath every five seconds. If moving the victim, give a few quick breaths prior to moving.

5 Determine if the victim has a pulse.
Check the pulse at the carotid artery (side of the neck) or femoral artery (groin) for at least twenty to thirty seconds.

6 If no pulse is detected, start cardiac compressions.

7 If the pulse returns, continue ventilation with rescue breathing as needed for as long as practical in a wilderness situation.

8 If a pulse does not return after twenty to thirty minutes of good effort, stop resuscitation efforts.
In wilderness areas far from medical care, prolonged basic CPR is of little use—the victim is unlikely to recover if they do not respond within the first few minutes.

HOW TO GET
TO THE SURFACE
IF YOUR SCUBA TANK
RUNS OUT OF AIR

1 Do not panic.

2 Signal to your fellow divers that you are having a problem—point to your tank or regulator.

3 If someone comes to your aid, share their regulator, passing it back and forth while swimming slowly to the surface.
Take two breaths, then pass it back to the other diver. Ascend together, exhaling as you go. Then take another two breaths, alternating, until you reach the surface. Nearly all divers carry an extra regulator connected to their tank.

4 If no one can help you, keep your regulator in your mouth; air may expand in the tank as you ascend, giving you additional breaths.

5 Look straight up so that your airway is as straight as possible.

6 Swim to the surface at a slow to moderate rate.
Exhale continuously as you swim up. It is very important that you exhale the entire way up, but the rate at

Keep your regulator in your mouth.

Keep your airway as straight as possible by looking toward the surface.

Swim at a slow to moderate rate, exhaling continuously.

which you exhale is also important. Exhale slowly—
do not exhaust all your air in the first few seconds of
your ascent. As long as you are even slightly exhaling,
your passageway will be open and air can vent from
your lungs.

WARNING: If you do not exhale continuously, you
risk an aneurysm.

Be Aware
• Never dive alone.
• Watch your pressure and depth gauges closely.
• Make sure your fellow divers are within easy
  signaling/swimming distance.
• Share a regulator in an emergency. It is much
  safer to use your partner's regulator than to try
  to make a quick swim to the surface. This is
  especially true the deeper you are, where you
  need to surface gradually.
• Always use an alternate air source instead of
  swimming up unless you are fewer than thirty feet
  below the surface.

THE EXPERTS

Foreword

Source: "Mountain" Mel Deweese, a Survival Evasion Resistance Escape Instructor, has trained military personnel and civilians to survive in all kinds of environments. He runs the Colorado Survival Skills Tipi Camp.

Chapter 1:
Great Escapes and Entrances

How to Escape from Quicksand

Source: Karl S. Kruszelnicki, Julius Sumner Miller Fellow at the School of Physics of the University of Sydney, Australia, the author of several books on physics and natural phenomena, including *Flying Lasers, Robofish,* and *Cities of Slime* and other brain-bending science moments.

How to Break Down a Door

Source: David M. Lowell, a certified Master Locksmith and Education/Proficiency Registration Program Manager of the Associated Locksmiths of America, an industry trade group.

How to Break into a Car
Source: Bill Hargrove, a licensed locksmith in Pennsylvania with 10 years of experience opening locks.

How to Hot-wire a Car
Sources: Sam Toler, a certified auto mechanic, demolition derby driver, and member of the Internet Demolition Derby Association; *Cartalk*, a weekly radio program on car repair broadcast on National Public Radio.

How to Perform a Fast 180-Degree Turn with Your Car
Sources: Vinny Minchillo, Internet Demolition Derby Association; Tom and Peggy Simons.

How to Ram a Car
Sources: Sam Toler (see above); Tom and Peggy Simons.

How to Escape from a Sinking Car

Sources: The U.S. Army's Cold Regions Research and Engineering Lab, located in New Hampshire; "Danger! Thin Ice," a publication of the Minnesota Department of Natural Resources; Tim Smalley, a boating and safety specialist at the Minnesota DNR.

How to Deal with a Downed Power Line

Source: Larry Holt, a senior consultant at Elcon Elevator Controls and Consulting in Prospect, Connecticut.

CHAPTER 2:
THE BEST DEFENSE

How to Survive a Poisonous Snake Attack

Sources: John Henkel, a writer for the U.S. Food and Drug Administration and a contributor to *FDA Consumer* magazine; Al Zulich, director of the Harford Reptile Breeding Center in Bel Air, Maryland; Mike Wilbanks, webmaster of the website Constrictors.com.

How to Fend Off a Shark
Sources: George H. Burgess, director of the International Shark Attack File at the Florida Museum of Natural History at the University of Florida; Craig Ferreira, board member, Cape Town's South African White Shark Research Institute, a nonprofit organization dedicated to research of the white shark and the preservation of its environment.

How to Escape from a Bear
Sources: "Safety Guide to Bears in the Wild," a publication of the Wildlife Branch of Canada's Ministry of Environment, Lands, and Parks; Dr. Lynn Rogers, a wildlife research biologist at Minnesota's Wildlife Research Institute and a director of the North American Bear Center in Ely, Minnesota.

How to Escape from a Mountain Lion
Sources: The National Parks Service; the Texas Park and Wildlife Association; Chris Kallio, backpacking guide for About.com; Mary Taylor Gray, a writer for *Colorado's Wildlife Company,* a publication of the Colorado Division of Wildlife.

How to Wrestle Free from an Alligator
Sources: Lynn Kirkland, curator of the St. Augustine Alligator Farm; Tim Williams of Orlando's Gatorland, who has worked with alligators for nearly 30 years and now lectures and trains other alligator wrestlers.

How to Escape from Killer Bees
Source: The Texas Agricultural Extension Service.

How to Deal with a Charging Bull
Source: Coleman Cooney, director of the Bullfight School.

How to Win a Sword Fight
Source: Dale Gibson, stuntman, teaches sword fighting skills to Hollywood actors and stunt people. He plays the knight in the Marine Corps commercials, and performed sword fighting stunts in *The Mask of Zorro.*

How to Take a Punch
Source: Cappy Kotz, a USA Boxing certified coach and instructor, and author of *Boxing For Everyone.*

CHAPTER 3:
LEAPS OF FAITH

How to Jump from a Bridge or Cliff into a River
Source: Chris Caso, stuntman, member of the UCLA gymnastics team and the U.S. gymnastics team, has produced and performed high-fall stunts for numerous movies, including *Batman and Robin, Batman Forever, The Lost World,* and *The Crow: City of Angels.*

How to Jump from a Building into a Dumpster
Source: Chris Caso (see above).

How to Maneuver on Top of a Moving Train and Get Inside
Source: Kim Kahana, stuntman, stunt director, and filmmaker. He has appeared in more than 300 films, including *Lethal Weapon 3, Passenger 57,* and *Smokey & the Bandit.*

How to Jump from a Moving Car
Sources: Dale Gibson (see above); Chris Caso, (see above).

How to Leap from a Motorcycle to a Car
Source: Jim Winburn, the director and stunt coordinator for two amusement park shows: "Batman" and the "Butch & Sundance Western Show."

How to Perform a Tracheotomy
Source: Dr. Jeff Heit, M.D., director of internal medicine at a Philadelphia area hospital.

How to Use a Defibrillator to Restore a Heartbeat
Sources: Dr. Jeff Heit, M.D. (see above); Tom Costello, district manager of Hewlett-Packard; Heartstream; the American Heart Association.

How to Identify a Bomb
Source: Brady Geril, vice president of Product Management for the Counter Spy Shops, the retail division of CCS International Ltd. of London. He is an expert in both survival products and tactics, and served as a supervising officer and undercover agent in the New York Police Department's narcotics division for 10 years.

How to Deliver a Baby in a Taxicab
Source: Dr. Jim Nishimine, M.D., obstetrician and gynecologist at Alta Bates Hospital in Berkeley, California. He has been delivering babies for 30 years.

How to Treat Frostbite
Source: John Lindner, director of the Wilderness Survival School for the Denver division of the Colorado Mountain Club, runs the Snow Operations Training Center, an organization that teaches mountain survival skills to power companies and search and rescue teams.

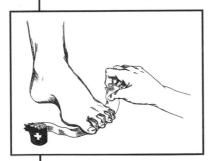

How to Treat a Leg Fracture
Source: Dr. Randall Simms, M.D.

How to Treat a Bullet or Knife Wound
Source: Charles D. Bortle, BA, RRT, NREMT-P, Paramedic and GMS Educator.

CHAPTER 5:
ADVENTURE SURVIVAL

How to Land a Plane
Sources: Arthur Marx, a pilot for more than 20 years, owns Flywright Aviation, a flight training and corporate flying service on Martha's Vineyard; Mick Wilson, author of *How to Crash an Airplane (and Survive!)* has a gold seal flight instructor certificate for both single- and multi-engine aircraft.

How to Survive an Earthquake
Sources: The U.S. Geological Survey; The National Earthquake Information Center.

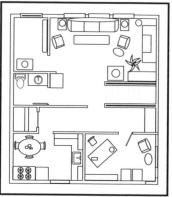

How to Survive Adrift at Sea
Source: Greta Schanen, managing editor of *Sailing Magazine,* has extensive experience both racing and pleasure cruising in deep water.

How to Survive When Lost in the Desert
Sources: The Arizona State Association of 4 Wheel Drive Clubs; *The Desert Survival Guide,* a publication of the City of Phoenix, Arizona.

How to Survive If Your Parachute Fails to Open
Source: Joe Jennings, skydiving cinematographer and skydiving coordination specialist. He has designed, coordinated, and filmed skydiving stunts for numerous television commercials, including Mountain Dew, Pepsi, MTV Sports, Coca Cola, and ESPN.

How to Survive an Avalanche

Source: Jim Frankenfield, director of the Cyberspace Snow and Avalanche Center, a nonprofit organization dedicated to avalanche safety education and information based in Corvallis, Oregon. Frankenfield has a degree in snow and avalanche physics and has led avalanche safety training for 10 years in Colorado, Montana, Oregon, and Utah.

How to Survive If You Are in the Line of Gunfire

Source: Brady Geril (see above).

How to Survive When Lost in the Mountains

Source: John Lindner, Colorado Mountain Club, director of the Wilderness Survival School (see above).

How to Make Fire Without Matches

Source: Mel Deweese (see Foreword, page 9).

How to Avoid Being Struck
by Lightning
Sources: John Lindner
(see above); The
Lightning Safety
Group of the
American Meteorological
Society; the National Weather
Service Forecast Office in Denver, Colorado.

How to Get to the Surface
If Your Scuba Tank Runs Out of Air
Source: Graham Dickson, Professional
Association of Diving Instructors (PADI)
Master scuba instructor.

the experts

ABOUT THE AUTHORS

JOSHUA PIVEN is a computer journalist and free-lance writer, and is a former editor at Ziff-Davis Publishing. He has been chased by knife-wielding motorcycle bandits, stuck in subway tunnels, been robbed and mugged, has had to break down doors and pick locks, and his computer crashes regularly. This is his first book. He currently makes his home in Philadelphia.

DAVID BORGENICHT is a writer and editor who has written several nonfiction books, including *The Little Book of Stupid Questions* (Hysteria, 1999) and *The Jewish Mother Goose* (Running Press, 2000). He has ridden in heavily-armored vehicles in Pakistan, stowed away on Amtrak, been conned by a grifter, broken into several houses (each for good reason), and has "borrowed" mini-bottles from the drink cart on Delta. He lives in Philadelphia with his wife—his best-case scenario.

Check out www.worstcasescenarios.com for additional survival tips, updates, and more. Because you just never know . . .